Amateur

An inexpert, inexperienced,
unauthoritative, enamored view of life.

The etymology of "amateur", "amatore", suggests someone who does something for love rather than money.

Author's Note:

Any reference to time across the book, "a month ago, a week ago", respects when the essay was written.

About Me

I am an amateur.

I love to read.

I love to write.

I love words. Finding the right one is like touching the sky.

I see metaphors for life everywhere.

I love food. I will always want to know what you had for dinner.

I prefer lemony or spicy over sweet. Green papaya salad over chocolate mousse.

I tell the truth as often and as clearly as possible.

There are people who had an impact on me who I no longer see. In most cases, I think that's a shame.

I am an introvert. If you knew me in person you'd find this impossible to believe.

I was raised religionless and don't know if there is a God.

I believe there is an indestructible kernel of divinity inside each of us.

I practice yoga. I meet myself there.

1

Whenever I had something good going and somehow sabotaged it, I concluded I had a self-destructive streak. I now realize my subconscious knows before I do when I am wrong to assume I have something good going. I have a self-preserving streak, and I trust it.

"Reliable" is my favorite compliment. (Failing that, I'll take "super hot".)

I will always look over my family. Even if they really, really don't want me to.

I learned to swim before I learned to walk. Being underwater fills me with a primal happiness.

I need space. If I can't get it, I become first distant, then insufferable. I wish I didn't.

I don't like parties. I go to great lengths to avoid them.

I feel lucky every day.

I feel grateful every day.

96% of the time, I love what I do for a living.

85% of the time, I like what I see in the mirror. The other 15%, I find solace in the fact that I have ridiculously pretty feet.

Breakfast is my favorite meal of the day.

I have an aversion to clutter.

I have no patience. I wish I did.

I used to believe that worrying somehow protected the people that I love. I now think worrying is a colossal waste of energy.

The life I have today exceeds all my expectations.

Old/New

When I was 14, a boy kissed me full on the lips under a porch light. The kiss was new until I found out he didn't have feelings for me and had kissed me on a dare. The edges of this kiss frayed before my eyes.

I married a guy when I was in my mid-twenties. We got back from our honeymoon and everyone told me we were newlyweds but I felt so old. The ring felt wrong, like a noose.

I married again in my early thirties. We worked and traveled and the jobs were shiny and the places were novel and for years it was wonderful until it wasn't. I knew it was time to let him go. I waved goodbye and now I see him and he's so happy. My brand new friend.

I now live in a dewy city, have a recent job, and live in a sparkling apartment with a hill I can walk to. My boyfriend and I have a five year anniversary coming up to which everyone says *"Five years! Wow! You guys aren't a new couple anymore!"* but they're so wrong. Just yesterday I climbed our hill to survey it all. Look. Shiny and radiant and beautiful. I just got here.

Plan For The Day

Two grungy men get on the bus and sit across from me. One has a small, battered suitcase.

"Here is what we'll do today" one of them says to the other. *"We will get off the bus. We will find a watering hole. We will get a big, cold beer."*

He opens a smidgen of the suitcase.

"And we will color."

He reveals dozens of coloring books.

"You will color inside the lines" he instructs. *"I will color outside the lines, and by end of the day we will see how each of us is feeling."*

He pulls out two packages of crayons from his jacket pocket. He hands one over.

"This is yours. It's new. All I did was throw out the pink one. I don't believe in pink."

Getting to overhear conversations like this one is the reason I don't drive to work.

A Thing With Substance

I can't tell you how many times I've heard *"I'll quit the day it stops being fun"*. Or *"it just wasn't fun anymore, you know?"*

For a long time this made sense, but upon further examination I've decided I don't buy into the fun principle.

While I do consider the pursuit of happiness should be central to everybody's life, I believe true happiness is a thing with substance.

The false sense that you "deserve better" ("deserve" — such a dangerous word!), that life is supposed to be a great big party, leaves me wanting.

More importantly, I believe that if I expected it to be that way I would set myself up to be regularly disappointed.

What I want, a lot more than laughs, to be amused or to be playful, is to live in a place (within myself) where I'm always learning.

Where the fear of failing at something is never what is guiding my decision to get involved in it or not.

Where I have people to love.

Even to be surrounded by things — simple, useful things — that I consider beautiful.

That seems worth sticking around for.

Better All The Time

Fact: everything changes.

Just like life can get worse, it can get better.

For me, life has gotten better. Indeed beyond what I ever imagined.

In hard times, here are some reflections that worked for me:

I don't do "master plans". People assure me *"you have to know what you want in order to find it"* but that's not how the best things I have in my life have arrived.

What yields the best results (for me) is to be open and receptive to the good things either already in front of me or as they present themselves.

This is how the outcome is usually an improvement over anything I could have designed.

If you plow towards something you miss everything else.

Don't wear blinders on your only adventure.

Besides, I don't always know what I want.

Or I find something and am amazed by how it wasn't really what I had in mind but it's...well. Perfect.

I am attracted to big moves. Give me a train ticket to anywhere. Let me sell all my things and move to another city. I will quit my job and start over.

Come on. You and me. Let's go.

But small changes are incredibly powerful and often a lot more viable.

Even when they don't seem connected to a traditional "life plan".

Even if you don't see how you can get there from here.

Small changes add up in ways you would never believe if you combine them with a receptive heart.

A few examples of small changes are: resolving to get really healthy (by eating better and exploring what that means to me), getting in shape, taking up a new form of exercise such as yoga or rock climbing, making it a point to read and write every day. Volunteering more, taking a few classes, traveling to places I have never visited, even if I don't leave my city.

If you only knew the places these changes have taken me. The people I have met.

Small things should be their own reward. Rather than doing something "because it makes sense" I do it because I am inexplicably drawn to it.

This is how the path I am on begins to curve towards more fortunate places.

Added bonus:
You can begin again with every breath. With every morning. You can begin again right after reading this.

Go ahead. Do it. Begin again.

Show Up

My younger brother, who lives in DC, recently broke his ankle. I flew from San Francisco to take him to the orthopedist.

For context, my brother is in his late thirties. He is the most mature, wisest, most level headed person I know.

He would roll his eyes at my claim that I "took him to the doctor" (or anywhere else.) He can take himself. He does not need my help.

In fact, I can confirm my presence in DC was largely useless.

But here is the thing: he's 8 years younger than me. He will always be my baby brother.

My family, siblings, friends and Boyfriend are all independent, intelligent people who manage perfectly well without my intervention.

As such, there is only one thing I can do for them: show up.

My plan is to keep doing so, despite the vehement protests I put up with.

Please, Sit

Setting: early evening. Crowded bus.

A woman sitting turns to a guy standing.

Her: *"Excuse me, would you like to sit here?"*

Him: *"Whah? Oh, no thank you."*

Her: *"I figured you could take my seat and I could sit on your lap."*

They regard each other for a second.

Him: *"Sure."*

I learn so much taking public transport.

Slapdash

I like symmetry and take great pleasure in lining things up.

Boyfriend is messy. He leaves black boots strewn across the living room floor, dirty dishes stacked in the sink, piles of indistinct things in nonsensical places.

Order soothes me.

Sometimes I get angry at Boyfriend for disrupting the alignment that I need to find in my apartment, a place where I can rest.

The more my life is out of my control (for example, when my father was very sick with dementia, leaving me scared, powerless, desperate) the more order I crave.

Life is chaotic and messy and leaves me feeling scratched and like nothing is in its place.

Organizing my things gives me the illusion of control.

My need for order is related to what I have going on inside me.

Boyfriend cannot be responsible for my often stormy internal weather.

There are other things too. Boyfriend does all the cooking. He makes fresh coffee and prepares a delicious breakfast for me, then leaves dishes in the sink because he needs to run to work.

He leaves shoes in the living room and things piled everywhere because it's his apartment too.

I like spotlessness. Boyfriend is slapdash.

I cannot demand that he be organized (or anything else that he isn't) to suit my requirements.

My need for order is my issue.

The two are unrelated.

The Ultimate Luxury

I love to sleep.

I am terrible at it. I have had insomnia since I was a little girl. Sleepless nights run in my family.

While night sleeping has always been a challenge — and a full night of uninterrupted sleep something I long for and seldom experience — I am particularly gifted at taking naps.

I used to think sleep was a waste of time and now believe it's one of the ingredients of a happy life. An afternoon spent napping is to me an afternoon well spent.

Hurray for naps.

Out Of Africa

I walk into my mother's room to let her know I've arrived safely.

She's lying in bed under the covers, with the cat on her chest. She's petting the cat and crying.

"Mom!" I say *"are you OK?"*

"Ugh" she responds, trying to breathe. *"I'm O.K. It's just that this movie is so, so sad".*

I turn to look at the television screen. I see words and a movie title.

"Mom" I tell her, *"it hasn't even started".*

"I know" she says, sobbing now. *"But I've already seen it".*

Silence

Setting aside quiet time (silence, space, peace) has always been the first step in correcting the course of my life.

When I set aside 20 minutes of silent time to think about where my life is going I begin to witness incredible change.

I find that everything I need is already inside me and that it sometimes gets diluted in a world of interference.

All I need to give myself is the opportunity to listen.

Added bonus —

If instead of using those twenty minutes to think I use them to breathe and just experience my deep, slow breaths — in, out, in, out — if I practice watching all my thoughts float by without holding on to them, then I can call it "meditation", and it changes everything.

Let's Hang Out. Go Away.

The first time I ever learned the definitions for an extrovert and an introvert, and how what defines each is the source of their energy, I considered it a revelation. I felt it provided a tidy, logical justification for so many things I didn't like about myself.

If I go overboard on the amount of time I spend with others I become insufferable — short tempered, impatient, depleted. After completing the Meyers Briggs test, I realized I rated high on the "introvert" scale. It shocked me. It explained everything.

I am often mistaken for an extrovert. I process many things, particularly of an emotional or logistical nature, out loud. I don't mind being the center of attention (that might be an understatement). I can be extremely chatty. I find humans delightful and strangers irresistible. I frequently interject in other people's conversations. (You know that person on the plane who talks to you even if you're pretending to read? That could be me. I apologize. But your book looks interesting. What made you pick it?)

I can also be very quiet, needing large swaths of time for myself, keeping my calendar free of social engagements for weeks. Recently, I was leaving my apartment, scurried into the elevator and quickly pressed (and pressed) the button for the ground floor. My boyfriend said it was impatient of me to not wait for the people behind us. "It's not that I'm in a rush" I whispered. "It's that I don't have the strength to say hello".

I would do pretty much anything to avoid a large party. The last one I was at was, alas, New Year's Eve at my house (long story). I asked people to leave two hours into the New Year and barely had enough strength to make it up the stairs to my bed. (I was vaguely worried I'd hurt their feelings, but a couple of days later they told me they were really impressed with how well I had done. See? Humans. Delightful.)

I have been known to leave a bar 6 minutes (not that I was counting) after I walk in if I determine it's too populated. I don't like having more than a handful of people over to my house at one time. It makes me feel I'd have nowhere to go if I needed a place to hide. I have a distaste for small talk that borders on aversion.

At work, I'm surrounded by people. They have gotten used to me saying things like "go away" as I see them approach my door. It's just that being interrupted is pure torture. When I get home at the end of a normal day I need space so badly I often sit in corner with no light, no book and no devices.

Many of the activities I enjoy the most are solitary by nature. Swimming. Reading. Writing. Yoga. When social plans are cancelled, what I feel, even when I really want to see the person in question, is relief. If a beloved friend calls from abroad announcing a visit and asks if she can stay at my apartment, I offer to pay for her hotel room. My friends know I'd do anything for them, anything, as long as they don't inadvertently threaten the room I need to retreat.

After being squarely extroverted and squarely introverted and pretty much every grade in between, I now believe there is nothing "better" or "wrong" about being either. We all have a possibility to be intermittently one or the other. To be one thing all the time — many of us are just not that clear cut. It can depend on the year, the weather, our mood, our caffeine intake, our glucose levels, our saturation point, the level of heartache we happen to find ourselves in and who knows what else.

Why does this matter? I often feel I need to recharge but have no inkling how to go about it. A book? A nap? Dinner? Learning where my ever-moving boundaries are is so much harder than I thought; but when I get things right I become a better person.

We all want to be better. We want to be spared the merciless spectacle that is to witness ourselves being resentful, snippy, petty. We don't want anyone to see what we look like when we are feeling overextended (I mean, it makes my hair look really frizzy).

I do public relations for a living. It's easy to jump to the conclusion that PR people are extroverts, but many of us like to write and ponder and research and do things that do not involve being in the midst of others (sometimes). Us introverts network well, thank you. Just one on one, rather than "working a room". We are smashingly inventive during a brainstorm, just not one that is taking place in the presence of others. And my observations on a document will be so much better if you give me the document. No, I don't want you to "walk me through it". And, tell me, why on Earth should we all have drinks after work if we've just spent the entire week together?

Recognizing our textured, beautiful complexity and getting to understand, respect and accept (ah, accept!) our ever changing, ever evolving, mercurial selves — resisting the temptation to throw anyone into a category, even after reviewing Meyers Briggs results — means I unlock the mystery of how not to put myself in a situation that will compromise me.

It means that even if it makes me feel selfish and like a terrible friend, maybe I shouldn't be throwing New Year's Eve parties at my place. It means, hopefully, that I will more frequently be able to smile to my neighbor in the elevator. And just as importantly, it means too that if on that plane trip my travel companion says he'd rather not talk, I nod knowingly and let him be.

Burrower

I thought I wanted to be a nomad
to fit all my possessions in a backpack
a traveler
a poet
speaker of seven languages
an existentialist
patriotic
a wanderer
adaptive
courageous
Instead I am a burrower
a lover of quiet evenings
rooted
a writer
a girlfriend
a daughter
an immigrant
solid
dependable
unmusical
yet completely in tune

Faking It

On this foggy, cold, rainy Sunday morning Boyfriend and I set the alarm at 7:00 a.m. to make it to the gym first thing.

I got out of bed and proceeded to loiter around the house and do a lot of things that weren't either necessary nor urgent.

Then I realized I was late and ran around in a panic, after which Boyfriend and I had the following text exchange:

Me: *"Good news — ran through rain and cold and successfully caught bus. Bad news: completely forgot to eat. I fear I need adult supervision."*

Boyfriend: *"Oh no. Where are we going to find an adult?"*

I don't think we ever start thinking like adults. I think everybody is faking it.

The Dog Of My Life

She was a rescue pit bull mix, all heart and muscle and strength and wild enthusiasm, and her name was Joy.

Joy saw me come home after a bad break-up and followed me around while I did nothing but cry.

I got into a car accident and had my arm in a cast for months and she'd sit near my bed, whimpering until I got up. She saw me dirty, sweaty, smelly, moody, depressed.

My multiple shortcomings made no difference to her.

When I put her outside, she'd do anything to get closer to me. She slammed against windows and would leap clear over a fence at the top of a flight of stairs. For her own safety I asked her repeatedly not to do that, and one day, distraught and exasperated, I took a newspaper and rolled it up and thwacked her with it for disobeying me. I haven't forgiven myself for that. She forgave me immediately.

Human love, while marvelous, is complicated. It's not that it isn't true: it's that we are so incredibly flawed. We adulterate it with what we bring with us. Our expectations and dreams and the promises we make and the judgments that taint us and (sometimes even inadvertently) our desire for things to be a certain way.

But when I'd see how Joy looked up at me with those honey-colored eyes so adoring and open and fearless, I knew she felt I was the best thing she had ever seen.

In her company I was a witness to the purest form of love.

Pink Diary

When I was little my mom's husband gave me a diary with a lock and key.

I wrote in it every day.

This didn't come from a place of discipline but rather a place of joy.

Writing is when all the dust settles. When starved, fleeting, fragmented, frazzled thoughts are pinned, cleaned, fed and enfolded. When noise and chaos turns to beauty and order.

When I sit down and write I feel most like myself.

I write because when I do I am at my happiest.

Four decades later, this is still my favorite part of the day.

Improbable

Boyfriend is Canadian and came to San Francisco from Montreal. I am Mexican and came to San Francisco from Mexico City.

He now claims that was the beginning of his willingness to always meet me a little more than half way.

We grew up in different countries and amid vastly different weather conditions. His years had four seasons and a very long winter. I grew up where it was always warm and spent most winters at the beach.

Growing up, when he spoke, he spoke in different languages than the ones I used.

He is the youngest son of a couple who remained married until death parted them. I am the oldest daughter of a couple who got divorced....more than once.

He was raised Jewish. I was raised religionless.

Boyfriend's dad had a single profession his whole life. My dad made a victorious career out of reinventing himself.

I often wonder where he was at different points in my life. I went to Montreal a couple of times before I met him, and he visited Mexico City long before he met me.

On our first date we discovered that our previous jobs — not one, but two — were in the same companies, in reverse order.

We also confirmed that for a whole year we worked in the same city, in the same building, one floor apart a few years before we met. We probably sent emails to the same people at the same time at corporate headquarters.

I now tell him I wish I could request the building's security videos for that year, just to get a visual of our crisscrossing trajectories.

We'd surely see us frequenting the same neighboring restaurants, brushing past each other in the lobby, getting into the same elevator at the same time; getting into different elevators, him going up, me going down.

My relationship with him is improbable. We are vastly different people. This equation was not supposed to add up the way it did. And yet it works.

The fact that we managed to find each other in the lobby of that hotel bar in an infinity of time and an infinity of space is a miracle, but it's not the one that astonishes me the most. It's that at this very moment he's making me dinner, and I'm here at my computer, and we occasionally turn and wrinkle our noses at each other.

It's the fact that we're here at all.

Loss

He saves everything. The proud way his parents looked at him when he took his first steps. His school uniform, the notes he wrote to others in class while the teacher wasn't looking. That box filled with old photographs, the sweater that belonged to his brother, his first love letter, the locket and the secret that it held. Later, records of every business card he ever received, unfinished plans, old formulas, proposals, even if they never saw the light of day.

She throws everything out. She doesn't take pictures, and what others take she rarely looks at. She gives books away after reading them, scribbles in notebooks she disposes of once the pages are full. His past is his treasure. Her life is a strong, clear line that does not look back and is scrubbed clean of the memories he finds solace in replaying before falling asleep. She has difficulty keeping friends. She does not attach meaning to objects; favors clean surfaces and empty spaces over buying a quilt that will remind her of that trip she took, back when everything was different to the way things are now. She does not believe in souvenirs.

They are the same, you see. He, terrified of losing something that was once his, if only for a moment, holds on to everything; she, convinced she can't lose what she doesn't have, holds on to nothing.

Elevating The Conversation

Growing up we held huge family meals on Sundays.

My Dad would regularly stand up and say *"This conversation has slipped below my standards. Let's elevate it."* We'd groan.

I now suspect this is the root cause of a tragic, awkward inability for me to engage in small talk.

No One Loses To Cancer

"You are the only person I've called" my father says. *"I have cancer".*

I knew right then I would lose him. But I didn't know I would lose him like I did, in installments. I was not prepared for the staggered, ruthless falling apart of one of the people I loved most in the world.

The man with a prodigious memory became forgetful. I don't mean he didn't know where he left his glasses. I mean he'd be angry for the fact we had not talked in weeks when in fact we had spoken that morning. He was always idiosyncratic but became contradictory, confessing he did not want to fight, did not want chemo; then scheduling appointments, and not showing up for them. He, never easy but frequently reasonable, became unwilling to adhere to any order by any doctor, refusing, for example, to take the antibiotics prescribed after a life-threatening surgery.

The man I knew as the most charismatic influencer became insatiably lonely. My superhero became afraid. Not just of death. Of life, of leaving his house, afraid of the dark. I could hear him pacing straight through the night. Ambition, diminished, gave way to restlessness. He lost all semblance of inner peace.

The strongest, frankly most dictatorial authority figure I have known would look at me blankly, unable to make even simple decisions. *"Tell me what to do"* he would say to the person he once instructed. *"I don't know what to do."*

"I have trouble imagining what the world will be like without me" he told me one day. *"I don't want to live in that world"* I replied. I meant it.

I looked at him while he was sleeping — a ghost of him, see-through almost — and began to cry, I hoped quietly. He opened his eyes and held my hand with his so very frail one, veins showing blue through his skin. I saw a faint, sweet glimmer of the ferocious protector he once was. *"Don't worry"* he patted me. *"This is nothing. I will recover."*

A few days later I overheard someone say a person they knew had "lost the battle" against cancer.

Lost? How can you lose after so many years well lived, after spending yourself every day in your endeavors, after being so impossible, after forging relationships with people you will come to count on, after reading so many books, after making your mark in so many different unsuspected places, after so much success, so much failure, after being such an active participant in this thing we call life?

That's when it hit me. Even our vernacular is all wrong when it comes to cancer.

I resent how cancer is represented.

Just because something kills you cannot possibly mean it defeats you. If that were true, we would all — masters and poets and liars and sinners and dancers and writers and heroes — be destined in the end to be losers.

I believe that my beautiful father is a winner who went, triumphant, to his own secular heaven, where he surveys the newspaper over freshly pressed coffee, eats delicious food, sips the best scotch, partakes in really good sex, jogs on a long beach, and spends a lot of time watching over the people he loved and left here, including me.

And cancer, deceiver, pretender, coward; it cannot even subsist without the vibrant people it depends on. It will end up shriveled up, dried up, dead; rolled up in dirty gauze and tossed into a wastebasket, quickly forgotten.

So suck it cancer. No one here will ever lose to you.

Explaining Sight To Someone Who Cannot See

When was the last time you looked forward to something, like a visit from a person you loved? Do you remember how you felt early on the morning of this anticipated occasion, the day you'd been waiting for stretched out immediately before you? That's green: the tight, certain potential of a bud.

On a hot day, walk in cool rain. The drops hitting your skin are what it feels like to see something sparkle. Each pelt holds a diminutive, delightful surprise, even as you're feeling it.

Listen to any song by Alicia Keys, all loud and full and scratchy. I think her music is red; insistent, impetuous, demanding. Red is hard to look away from and it likes it that way. It's always such a show-off.

After a generous, salty dinner, hold something cold and sweet in your mouth, like watermelon or an orange. That's what yellow feels like; a burst of refreshing energy that lifts your spirits without being saccharine or tiresome.

After a noisy day, sit in a room alone. Not sad alone. Not longing alone. Peace alone. That's blue; quiet, spacious suspension. The sky is blue. People who see could look up and escape any time, but we forget we can so we almost never do.

Cover yourself with a soft blanket and trace the contours of your own shape lying under it. That's what the hills of California look like, gentle curves that slope for miles, giants sleeping under blankets of hay.

After a long night of restless sleep yank open a window and feel the outside air blow in and replace the stale one. That's what the The Golden Gate Bridge feels like, standing clean and proud as it guards the entrance of The San Francisco Bay.

The Difference Between Tenacious And Stubborn

The difference is Boyfriend's disposition.

Boyfriend happy with me: *"Dushka. You are so tenacious."*

Boyfriend irritated at me: *"Ack, Dushka. You are SO STUBBORN."*

Joking aside, the exact same quality tends to be both our strength and our weakness.

Within what makes us powerful lies what could be our undoing (and vice-versa.)

For example, I can indeed be, ummm, really tenacious.

Don't tell Boyfriend I said so.

The Luckiest Person

I am not afraid to say that I believe I am the luckiest person on Earth.

Well, OK. I am afraid. Very afraid.

Truth be told, the fact that I sometimes feel this way kind of freaks me out.

The thoughts that race through my head are: *"Why? Why me? Whatever did I do to deserve such a huge amount of blissful blessings?"*

And, perhaps more importantly, *"when is the other shoe going to drop,"* in the manifestation of some calamity?

Will my luck run out? Will my good fortune change course? (For a while there I believed it had. I don't wish hopelessness on anyone.)

I've decided that I have a choice. I can torture myself with the thoughts in the paragraph above. Take in my luck and react to it with panic, with a sense that I might lose everything at any moment (which is always possible). And in doing so, successfully jeopardize the delight derived from what is bestowed upon me.

But, wouldn't this be the clear opposite of gratitude?

Or, (gasp) I can assume that there is a reason I am this lucky, and that someone somewhere somehow determined that I am worthy of it.

(To whom it may concern: thank you.)

I believe every being on the planet deserves abundance and good fortune, so, why not me?

So today (and every day) I make the decision to not allow myself to be stressed by what life grants me.

Instead, I will let this enormous feeling of gratitude that I carry with me wash over me, in a ritual at least as frequent as my daily shower.

And relish every gift that comes my way, and honor the bestower by doing so with a thankful, awed, open heart.

It Doesn't Matter

It doesn't really matter

All the things I remember
How my father would carry me on his shoulders
My mother's box of rings
The miniature Eiffel tower
The manta rays swimming in the light of the dock

Everything becomes a footnote
Something someone puts in parenthesis
Or leaves in the back of a closet

(remember how I said I liked your tie?)

Or has to figure out how to dispose of
After you're no longer here

My Dad

The first time I tasted Scotch I was teething. My Dad used it to soothe my gums.

When I was seven he taught me how to say *"le mots impossible n'existe pas"* because he wanted his kid to quote Napoleon.

He loved women. When I was ten he explained that infidelity was a requirement for the procurement of the species and that, as such, monogamy was an absurd social construct.

He did not teach me how to ride a bicycle, drive a car or throw a ball but he did tell me that reading was the most important thing I could be doing with my time.

He never remembered my birthday and asked me the same questions over and over because he didn't pay attention enough to retain very much of what I told him.

When I called to say my then husband and I were splitting up before I even explained what had happened he blurted *"Call him and ask him to forgive you."*

There wasn't anyone like my Dad. He made me feel safe and I grew up convinced that between good and evil, good would always win.

Through A Stranger's Eyes

We tell ourselves things and repeat them until we believe them. You know. I am trapped. My life is over. I am unlovable. I have become invisible.

I suppose that if I told myself the opposite with the same tenacity I would eventually believe it too. Your life is just beginning. Anything is possible. Inside you is everything you need.

It was early Saturday morning, and I was in my sunny, one bedroom apartment. After much practice I was stretched out in the very center of the bed, using every pillow. I was living alone for the first time in more than 15 years. And I was pondering where exactly one goes from here.

I'm afraid the story is not terribly original. I used to be married to my best friend. We moved to the U.S. together from different countries and worked in the same company for most of my adult life. This meant that every person I knew, every friend, every co-worker, every client, knew us as a unit. It felt like every road led back to him.

I had a clear sense that I needed to start over. But how does one go about doing that at 42? How could I meet people I wouldn't normally come across? How could I gain access into different walks of life?

The answer came to me suddenly. I swallowed. Online dating.

Up until now I had regarded online dating with disdain. I felt it zapped romance out of the equation, extracted serendipity and left you with something clinical and contrived and similar to a work interview.

Not to mention, I had not dated for over 20 years.

Right. So online dating would be the way to stop doing what I had always done, which might, if one follows logic, give me a shot at a different result.

On with it, then.

To keep things simple, I decided to focus on a single site and picked OK Cupid.

I found myself struggling with the most fundamental parts of the questionnaire, such as the ability to distinguish what I liked versus what "we" liked. It occurred to me that defining myself to strangers would be an effective exercise in reconstituting who I was.

After a few days of tentative practice and a slow "waiting to be discovered" approach, I arrived at a notion that took precedence over the hard to get frame of mind I had grown up with. If I waited for people to notice my profile and contact me, the universe of those I could choose from would shrink considerably. I much preferred picking from anyone I wanted, even if it meant risking sometimes not getting a reply.

Another realization: My end game wasn't finding love. What I yearned for was a new life, a fresh perspective. My criteria would have to change accordingly. Instead of asking myself *"Is this person boyfriend/husband material?"* I would remind myself to ask *"would going out with him be interesting? Fun? Would I learn something?"*

I organized my days like this: I'd get up very early and go into work. I'd leave to go to the gym. Then, I'd go out on a date. I'd be asleep before 11:30 pm.

I met someone new every day for about a month. Because I was so fed up with being in a state of emotional paralysis. Because I knew that somewhere out there was a world too rich to warrant the delusion that I was finished. But mostly because I quickly learned that everyone was interesting, and that everyone had something to teach me.

I dated a man who taught me that there is rhythm in chaos through listening to jazz, which I had previously written off as lowly elevator music. I met an engineer who spent an evening patiently proving to me that pool was infallible if I played it right (*"See? It's mathematical."*)

I reached out to a drummer and asked if he would give me a few lessons. *"I will meet you at the park at 1:30"* I wrote. *"I will be wearing yellow sneakers"*. *"Great!"* he replied *"I'll be the one with the Mohawk"*.

I went out on a date with a motorcycle repairman who had a Master's Degree in poetry from Yale. He offered to take me for a ride in the desert under the light of the full moon.

I saw a DNA expert who in explaining the miracle implicit in the double helix reminded me I was impossible to replicate. I met a man who started his own non-profit and claimed to be fluent in Spanish. When I switched to that language he looked irritated and said he refused to do anything on cue.

I sat on a dock overlooking the water, eating a picnic with a man who grew up in a traveling circus and was raised by mimes. I met a mechanic who specialized in European automobiles. *"If foreign cars are your specialty"* I reasoned *"then you must have a knack for handling high maintenance women"*. *"Are you high maintenance?"* he countered. *"Absolutely"* I said.

I sat at a coffee shop with a man who had been sailing for seven years and had just returned to dry land. I asked him how many countries he had visited. *"Visit countries?"* he asked, perplexed.

"Why would I do that?" "Well then" I pressed on *"I bet you really got to know the people you were sailing with".* *"It was just two of us"* he said. *"One of us slept while the other sailed, so we seldom exchanged a word".*

I met an artist who worked all year to spend his annual salary creating a monument sized sculpture he would transport to an art festival in the middle of a dry lake bed, only to burn it down. He said it was the constant reminder he needed of how ephemeral life is, how beautiful and how pointless.

I read a guy's profile which sounded less like he was looking for a date, more like he was trying to find religion. *"Reach out"* he wrote *"if you think you have answers".* Over tea I told him I had recently learned how futile it was to plan. *"We can't predict what we want, as it assumes we're not going to change. The future has so many variables we can't see that the most accurate way to live our life is to go by what would make us happy right now."*

He sat there looking at me. He then told me he had survived a terminal cancer diagnosis 8 years before, and had found out a couple of days ago that it was back. *"I don't want chemo again"* he said. *"What should I do?"* I stood and put my arms around him and we held each other there, in the middle of a French café, two strangers who had the answers to nothing.

One guy mentioned he loved cooking and couldn't live without a good chef's knife. He wrote out a few lines of an Elvis Costello song describing a woman wearing elbow length gloves. I thought going out with someone *"with a healthy relationship to debauchery and excess"* would make for a fun evening. *"Reach out if you think you can beat me at arm wrestling"* he wrote.

"I can beat you at arm wrestling" I assured him. *"And I bet you anything you can't do a headstand".*

"That is really bold for someone who's never met me" he replied. *"What are we betting?"*

"We'll do the headstand challenge first" I said. *"If I lose, I will buy*

you a knife. If I win, I want a pair of elbow length gloves. So I can wear them as I beat you at arm wrestling."

He showed up to our first date with a pair of black velvet elbow length gloves that fit me perfectly.

In his version of the story I lost the bet. In my version I won, because he is here, making me coffee as I write this. We have been living together for over a year.

I've never met anyone like him. He is an original, with a sparkling, transparent heart I can see right through; a solid character with a penchant for bacon and Manhattans and what I hope is an incorrigible tendency to hog all the pillows.

What astonishes me is that I never would have found the man currently known as Boyfriend had I not gone out of my way to reach out to people I expressly considered not to be boyfriend material.

What He Needed

Two men stand in the crowded bus.

One carries a guitar, the other a briefcase.

Every time the first strums, the second glares. *"This is an enclosed public place. If you do that again I will break your fingers".*

After a few stops, he storms off.

The man with the guitar picks tentatively. He plays softly at first, then fills the bus with a simple, clean, beautiful piece.

I get off feeling so peaceful; and sad for the man with the briefcase.

He missed out on exactly what he needed.

Male/Female

In Spanish, everything has a gender.

In English, for example, you say "passion"; in Spanish you say *"la pasión"*.

This is how I know passion is female.

Love, *el amor*, is male, as is the kiss.

Loneliness and promises are both female. So are patience, family, food, and thirst. Hunger is male.

Arrogance is female, pride is male.

Sin and deceit are male. Lies are female.

Drama is male, as is horror, terror and fear. Protection is female. Safety is female.

The night is female, as is darkness, light, the stars and the moon. The lake — assuming there is a lake — is male. So is the ocean. Clouds and waves are female.

Intelligence is female, as is life, history, the mind, poetry and literature. Essays and stories are male. So are thoughts, and work. Dedication is female.

Planet Earth is male, and so is the color green, the color blue and the sun. The galaxy that contains them all is female.

The notebook I scribble in is male, as is the pencil I use. The computer is female.

The world is male. Beauty is female, as are dichotomy, truth and treason.

Hope and faith are both female. Forgetting is male.

Questions are female, as are my answers, or any answers.

Already Perfect

Me: *"I spent the entire night frantically looking for a place to alter a dress."*

Boyfriend: *"You mean, in your dream?"*

Me: *"Yes."*

Boyfriend: *"And then what?"*

Me: *"I finally found the right tailor but when I lay the dress on the glass counter it didn't need anything done."*

Boyfriend: *"You know what that means."*

Me: *"No."*

Boyfriend: *"That everything is already perfect just the way it is."*

Boyfriend. Dream interpreter.

Malevolent Plot

The holidays — the whole lot of them — are part of a malevolent plot to bring introverts to their knees, thinly disguised as continuous, joyful celebration.

Here are some evil-genius ingredients:

Forced fun. The prime, most beastly example of this is New Year's Eve (The hats. The sparkle. The bubbles. The countdown.) But really the same goes for all the others: yes, you Halloween, even with your abundance of chocolate and your colorful sugar bounty.

You too, Thanksgiving, with your crispy turkey and irresistible sides.

Lots of people you love, in the same place at the same time. You can't talk to just one or two of them. You *want* to be able to talk to all of them. You simply don't have the mental stamina.

Lots of people = increased likelihood for small talk. No. No. I don't know what to say to you. I'll just nod. Nod. Nod.

Lots of people in confined spaces. You want to hide in the bathroom but someone is already in there.

Lots of people in confined spaces who tend to either stay over or encourage you to stay over. This means one thing: there is nowhere to recharge. And there is no light at the end of the tunnel. And social exhaustion is cumulative, so by the end of the year all you want is to roll up in a ball and cry. (Joking aside, this is what I was doing last year on New Year's Eve: I was rolled up in a ball on my couch, crying.)

Lots of people who HAVE TO SEE YOU! BEFORE THE END OF THE YEAR! It wasn't urgent in June to see you before August, but it sure is urgent now.

Lots of people. Sigh.

Incredibly meaningful dates so that if you decline, you miss something important that you later feel crappy about.

I adore my family. I adore my friends. I want to spend time with them.

But I don't want to be at my worst when I do.

Here are some things I do (with varying degrees of success.)

I say no. I miss tons of important parties. I'm sorry beloved people. This is about my survival.

I prioritize. There are certain things I don't miss.

I never stay over at anyone's house, and I love you but you can't stay at my apartment. Not over the holidays, not ever.

I have a boyfriend who understands me. He often goes to parties without me, representing both of us (or so I tell myself.) And when I do go and say *"sweet love, maybe it's getting to be time to go?"* he (usually) knows I mean *"CODE RED. EXTRACT."*

I have friends who understand me. *"My inner introvert needs some attention"* I say.

Yup. I believe we are, each of us, strong enough to deactivate the most heinous, elaborate conspiracy.

The Final Blow

Someone once explained dementia to me like this:
You frequently forget where you left your keys. That's human.
You have the keys in your hand and you look at them and you cannot put together what they are or what they do. That's dementia.

You can (and do) take notes meant to remind yourself of what you know you are forgetting. Then you stare at the notes unable to recognize what they mean.

My Dad had dementia. In its early stages he said he felt "confused". He looked disoriented.

As it progressed it felt to the rest of us like an exacerbation of his personality: his tendency to repeat things, him being obstinate, difficult. He was loving and impossible but he always had been so maybe this was just him getting old.

Then it was all fear. Paralyzing distress at anything that altered his routine, accusations that seemed like there was no soothing him. *("You never call me." "But, we spoke less than an hour ago".)*

When you begin to lose your memory you also lose order. In your mind there is no chronology. You hear children playing outside. Are they your friends coming over to play? Or, have years gone by and they are your kids? Or, your grandkids? Where are you? Who are the people in the faded photographs?

He knew all along he was losing his mind. We talked about it, devised plans, agreed on treatment. He promised he'd go get tests, go to the doctor. He would then forget every conversation, and refuse to follow through. A man without memory cannot keep his word. His word, once the most sacred thing.

Right to the very end, as his brain got more tangled and became mirrors and delusions and smoke, I could still clearly see him underneath, that incredible mind, his sense of humor, his startling, startling intelligence. And his love. He loved me.

You can't "overcome" dementia. It's like you being a witness to someone taking an eraser and slowly obliterating your outlines, then who you are. Every superhero knows this day will come, and here it is. Your kryptonite.

Dementia is not "awkward". It's merciless. It's relentless. It's incurable. And it will take its time to kill you.

Once that's done it delivers the final blow: the people you loved and were unfailingly there for will struggle to remember what you used to be before dementia first arrived.

Not Poetry

Loose sentences
No punctuation
Or solid thought
dust
does not constitute poetry

a poet has a serious job
reports on the blue cup she uses at breakfast
the old copper coin she finds in the grass
the flower that grows right through the pavement
the silver spoon with the delicate white handle
the bruised pear in the fruit bowl
the key once essential that no longer opens anything
how a stranger looks from behind and from a distance

this is just debris

Unexpected Twist

A few years ago, over breakfast, my Dad told me that at 20 he had his life mapped out, including a nice girl he'd marry.

Except a woman unlike anyone he'd ever known was about to appear on the scene. She was larger than life and would forever change the course of his destiny.

And she would give him me.

Hurray for indomitable moms and unexpected twists in the futile plans we make.

Like A Horse

It's a recurring dream. Or rather, a recurring interruption of whatever it is I'm dreaming. A presence somewhere over my shoulder, a nuzzling on my neck. Like a horse, its hot, moist breath, the brush of its velvet lips. Except that the smell is not animal-like. It's more like warm bread, nutmeg and bed linens. Then a stream of sound I can't make out — a radio frequency?

This happens almost every night for as long as I can remember. I've grown so used to it it doesn't occur to me to wonder what it means.

It takes me seventeen years to finally understand. It's a human voice, deep and lush, and it's saying something. It's words, and they are clear and eloquent, if somewhat redundant, like a mantra. And they are in English (I grew up in Mexico, so words in English can only mean one thing.)

"You are the most precious, beautiful girl in the world," the voice is saying. *"There is nothing you can't do. You are a miracle. You are here against all odds. You are here for a reason. You are going to change the world."*

The words begin to irritate me, because I'm so tired and they just keep coming. I feel exactly the way you do a few seconds before you gather the strength to finally reach out for the snooze button.

I tighten my eyes shut, crunch up my shoulder against my neck, hoping. It. Will. Go. Away.

It doesn't. The fourth *"There is nothing — nothing — you can't do"* finally does it. I'm now fully awake. I open my eyes and in the dark make out my mother's figure, kneeling on the floor in her nightgown, her elbows on the edge of my bed, her mouth grazing my ear. I roll back, alarmed.

"Mom!" I say, *"What are you doing?"*

"I didn't mean to wake you." She says this kind of unapologetically. *"I'm just whispering things in your ear."*

Like this is perfectly logical.

"What kind of things? I mean, you woke me up! I was sleeping, mom!"

"I say things to you while you sleep so they will go directly into your subconscious." Her tone is clinical, like when a doctor says *"I'm afraid this will require antibiotics." "I didn't mean to wake you. I guess I was talking a bit louder than I usually do."*

"What do you mean 'usually'?"

"Go back to sleep, honey" she says and backs out of the room. *"I'll see you tomorrow."*

His Remains

My father died the 15th of December, 2014. After his death my siblings and I remained in his house through the holiday season, in the rooms we used to sleep in when we were children.

We spent the strange, hollow days that followed huddled around the table in his library.

In my darkest hour — facing my life without my father — I never felt alone, or unsupported, or misunderstood.

My father left me surrounded by people who felt exactly like I did.

This feeling carried through the following year. While my siblings and I have always been close, in our own individual ways we have grown closer.

In a recent call with one of my brothers he made the exact same comment my father would have made. When I pointed it out we both laughed.

Finding delightful snippets of my father lovingly wrapped in the people who bolster me has been the best thing he left behind.

Not Disposable

Deciding to remain friends with my ex-husband is one of the most important decisions we ever made.

As we began the divorce proceedings we recognized divorce was, at its most fundamental, a solution, not a problem.

We vowed to put each other first.

Many close friends told me that it would be healthier for us to let each other go.

But, wait. How many people in the world do you come across who are not blood related that you consider family?

Why would you ever discard something that priceless?

Humans like neat labels. "Husband". "Boyfriend". "Friend".

What if what's true has no name? What if there is no word for what we are?

I cannot live by what others are comfortable with. I have to live by what works for me.

So my ex-husband, beloved friend, is my family. We went through 15 years of marriage together, and we survived divorce.

We rode smoothly through financial decisions (instead of fighting over stuff the conversation would go like this: Him: *"You love this. You should keep it."* Me: *"No, you should definitely take it."*)

We suffered through the unpredictable collateral damage that divorce brings. (People around you react in odd ways and you end up losing friends for inexplicable reasons. This is one of the things about divorce no one talks about: the unexpected riptides and undercurrents that throw you off when you're already off kilter.)

We held hands as we signed our divorce papers. His was the shoulder I cried on when our divorce was final.

He was the person who helped me find a new apartment when we decided (for logistical reasons) it make sense for him to stay in the house we lived in.

Some time later, we made a point to introduce our new significant others to each other early on. When Boyfriend met ex-husband we had been dating about a month. *"After seeing you together"* Boyfriend said *"I know you will be friends for the rest of your life. I understand."*

Remaining friends with your ex is not only possible. Sometimes, in the middle of the heartbreak and chaos that is life, it's the only decision that makes any sense.

Don't Mince Words

Once upon a time I was struggling with a job I wasn't getting done. I was telling my best friend how frustrated I felt.

Her: *"Why don't you quit?"*

Me: *"Because I don't want to walk away feeling like I suck. I want to figure it out and leave feeling that I did what I set out to do."*

Her: *"That makes sense. Good luck letting your ego make your decisions."*

Three cheers for friends who don't mince words.

Rituals

When I was a little girl my mom told me that using body cream was very important. I don't remember how old I was; I must have been six or seven. I have a clear memory of watching her slather it on her legs, then hold the open jar in front of me so that I would do the same. Putting on cream is something I do every day right after I get out of the shower. All these years I've never questioned if I need to do it or if my skin is dry. It's automatic, like brushing my teeth or pulling the sheets up over my ears.

It was my father who taught me the importance of drying my feet thoroughly and running the corner of the bath towel back and forth between my toes after every shower. I remember him declaring, in that inarguable way of his, that water between my toes was bad for me. (He explained it could cause the skin to split, which to this day makes me wince). When I get out of the shower, I indeed take the corner of the towel and run it back and forth between each toe (somewhat obsessively — I wonder where that came from?), even when I'm in a mad hurry. I can guarantee it: no residue of humidity on my feet, ever.

It's odd, the bits of programming our parents leave in us.

It occurred to me recently that these two rituals ensure I start each day with the omnipresence of the two people who love me most in the world.

A gift of deep caring, all wrapped and handed to me every morning before I even make it out of my house.

Borges, John Lennon, and Me

There is nothing I can write — no possible combination of all words in the vast vocabulary that is the English language — that hasn't been written before. Nothing I can cook or eat, do or say, or even think. It's not merely that it's all been done, it's that I'm afraid it's all been done by me. By past versions of me. I'm not even the original me.

Jorge Luis Borges reasons that if time is infinite, and the universe is infinite, and the number of possible combinations that result in a person and in a situation they find themselves in is immense, but finite, then one can logically deduce that it all happens more than once.

I will at some point in the past or the future again be born to the same parents. My father will again hold my hand in his as we stroll through the flower market. My mother's husband will teach me how to string beads into necklaces while we sit on a white carpet.

My mother will again take me to far away places every summer and gallop off into the desert on a black Arabian horse.

I will hate school again, flunk every possible subject again, be betrayed by my best friend, be grossed out by my first kiss, dream of having long hair, again organize my books on the shelves in my room in a certain order that is really a code.

A dog will walk into my life and I will call her Joy and I will never love another dog that way again, until it's her again and me again.

I will buy a small blue table to work on, do again all the things I swore I'd never do and leave everything for love. I will find my way to California and decide painfully, inexorably, that it is home.

Some day, in the future and the past, I will be sitting at this computer alone just like I am now coming to the realization that there is nothing I can do that can't be done.

Sometimes the thought is freeing. If it's all been done before, then worry is an illusion. There are no mistakes. I'm along for a ride that is the story of my life.

Sometimes the theory renders me powerless. Is time nothing more than a series of concentric circles, a cosmic helix, a spiral we move through again and again, like water draining out of a bathtub?

Are we all trapped into learning the same lessons even after we've learned them, having to tolerate the same people we will never understand, traveling to the same places as if they were new? It's not possible then to truly leave a mark or to do anything of any real consequence.

Or, every infinitesimal decision carries more weight than I ever considered, as I will be condemned to play it out again and again across billions and billions of years.

Mistakes I Make More Than Once

Letting my ego make the call. It's really hard to recognize it and silence it. (I try to let more important things be my guide: teamwork, love, results, the greater good, the lesson, anything.)

Believing that other things, such as being comfortable with a job I already know how to do, are more important than learning. I am so much happier when I'm learning.

Being in a hurry. So many mistakes I make I can trace back to being in a rush. Slow down.

Thinking I can multitask. I can only do one thing at once. Remind me.

Personal Furnace

Late at night when my feet are cold I press them up against Boyfriend. Nothing ever wakes him up and he is like a personal furnace.

I wonder if he sometimes dreams that he walks through icy swamps.

I snuggle up against him with freezing hands and smell him.

I wish I could bottle his smell.

I'd never be afraid.

As I snuggle I very gently wedge myself into the spot he is sleeping on. Double warmth.

Sometimes in the morning he wonders why he sleeps so fitfully.

I shrug.

Food, Glorious Food

I think my mother and I used to make bread together. I imagine her, sifting and measuring and wiping everything down, me sinking my hands into various "wet" or "dry" mixtures and squishing the contents through my fingers.

I don't remember the actual act of making bread, but to this day the sight, smell and feel of flour remind me of her and the efficient, full fledged production that was her cooking.

I do remember my mother used to make Christmas bread for her friends. Obstinately believing holiday gifts should not be bought but made, she'd spend five days and nights in the kitchen, baking over 500 loaves of bread that would then be individually wrapped. Afterwards, she'd resentfully swear she'd never do it again and, still covered in flour and smears of yummy smelling goo, she'd slip her stained oven mitts on one more time and yank a loaf fresh out of the oven, bang on the bottom of it and shake the contents onto a rack on the counter. She'd cut thick slices of it, and we'd eat it with our fingers, without even sitting at the table. A few minutes later she'd take a gulp of coffee, declare the ordeal officially over and go to bed.

Paris. My father took me there for the first time when I was seven. I know we went with a lot of other people, but I see only him and me at that tiny, candlelit table for two. He taught me how to take a mini-pancake from the basket, set it on the plate, put caviar on it, and slowly place it in my mouth. Soon, the pancake basket — plate — caviar bowl — pancake — mouth process became a two step caviar bowl — mouth frenzy while he pretended not to notice. I haven't had caviar since. Why interfere with that perfect marine memory?

Early morning. Bread and fruit in Naxos. I'd leave the room we were staying at, go to the market before anyone else was up, order bread and fruit in Greek (between you and me, I mostly just pointed), pay, count the coins, say *efharisto* and take everything back to the room. It was my first taste of independence (I can go downstairs, up the street and into the market, alone) and empowerment (I can make myself understood, anywhere. Ergo, I can do anything.) I'd return, triumphant, generously spreading out the goods on the bed and giving back the correct amount of change. Making our parents proud fulfills the most basic, most insatiable of needs.

Pepper steak, somewhere on the coast of France. I didn't know pepper could be not pepper, not a pungent, dark dust but a buttery, wood colored sauce. And so....well, peppery. I don't like meat that much anymore, but pepper steak has a place in my heart. When I see it on a menu, I never fail to pause and greet it.

When I was maybe eleven, I had a friend, Maru, who had a permanent stash of "American candy" at her disposal. Her parents would travel to the US frequently, and bring back whole suitcases of loot (And Agree shampoo). I would go over to her house and we'd set up a tent in their garden, then go through an obscene amount of sugar (Fun Dip and Milky Way remain clearest in my memory.) Junk food was sacrilege at my house. I didn't want Maru to know I was breaking such an uncool rule, so I would tell her that I would be picked up 10 minutes before the real pick up time. I'd say goodbye, then spend that frantic moment rinsing my mouth and my fingers with the hose in her garden. I'm sure my mother noticed my purple tongue despite my efforts to conceal the evidence — besides which, I must have been bouncing off the walls. Today, I unfailingly stare at the rows and rows of candy at the supermarket. I don't buy any — I don't even want to. But I'm irrevocably attracted to the bright colors and delicious excess of the displays.

Panzerotto in Duvrovnik, on a small, rickety white table overlooking the Mediterranean. My ex-husband later explained, in a mildly offended tone, that panzerotto was Italian. He took me to a place where they make them behind Piazza del Duomo. Yup. Same gorgeous, golden, bubbly stuff. So good, it did not let down my recollection of it, which had remained untouched for more than 20 years.

Tabouleh and hummus at my Godmother's house. She was Lebanese and everything about her radiated a sophistication I could never quite belong to. The flowing hair. The silk robes. The white fluffy rugs. The low furniture. Having a meal while sitting on the floor. And, hummus! Who knew that could be done with a chick pea? To this day I don't eat it without thinking of my Godmother who, somewhere in heaven, must be appalled that I still leave the house without a lick of make-up on.

Noodles in China. I sat in a sort of stall in the streets of Xian, watching a man roll, then stretch out the dough, slice it magically into noodles against his arm, after which he'd throw it into a huge, steaming bowl. He'd proceed to serve generous portions of it, and I could barely see his slim face and straight, black hair through the clouds of steam. Those noodles were spicy, hot and worth a trip back to China, which I plan to do.

The first time I ever had pasta al aglio, oglio e peperoncino. My then husband put an apron on, chopped, measured, timed, drained and put it into a serving dish, which he set with flair on the center of the table. As I ate, I thought *"A man who cooks. With an apron. I think I love him.".* When I looked over, he was looking at me, wide eyed. *"What are you thinking?"* I asked, hopefully. *"You just ate nine servings of pasta"* he responded. (To his credit, he wasn't horrified. He was in awe.). I thought the power of pure, true love would make me immune to caloric consumption. (It didn't).

Risotto alla parmigiana in a hole in the wall by the side of the road near Aosta. Pretty much everything I've eaten in Italy belongs on this list, but that risotto again proved to me that you don't need much of anything to make a meal good.

Burrata. The most fresh, most creamy dish ever created. "Fresh" is usually used to describe vegetables, leafy greens, fruit. "Creamy" is rich. It's mouth feel and often heavy. This is fresh and creamy and light, with a clean aftertaste, not greasy. I seem to have a natural affection towards any dish that comes from Puglia. I'm afraid to visit.

Cremini FIAT. The best chocolate. Ever. This from someone who likes to try new things and who consumes chocolate regularly. When I made a trip to Italy (which used to happen rather frequently as I was married to an Italian), I buy a box or two of Fiat *"to take home and savor across several months"*. The boxes never saw the inside of my suitcase.

Chile covered mango. So reminiscent of my childhood and adolescence. In Mexico, you eat tamarind covered in chile, lollipops covered in chile, gum covered in chile and even just chile with sugar. I'd found nothing like it in the US, until I came across this chile encrusted dried mango from Trader Joe's I can't open without feeling my mouth water.

And of course the list would not be complete without a loving nod to the Indian food I tasted on my trips to India. *Sambar* and *biryani* and *raita, dosas* and *idilis*.

So much incredible food I've eaten and forgotten to mention. So many dishes I have yet to taste. So many places I still need to visit.

It's For My Brain

I go to the gym almost every day (five times a week.)

For me, the benefits are mental. A clearer head, a calmer disposition, increased definition in my thinking, more focus. Diminished stress, less worry and anxiety.

Without it, my brain is a very very noisy place.

I credit my alleged sanity to the fact that I exercise.

Everything else — from a stronger heart to firmer muscles to a fit body — is a welcome bonus.

Every Bit of Me

My Dad and I are bantering over dinner.

Dad: *"Just don't lose sight of the fact that you are my creation."*

Me: *"Well, mom did play a role in the matter."*

Dad: (Grins.) *"Please. It was all me. She was just the means of transport."*

While I see how this might antagonize any mother, I find it adorable that someone loves me fiercely enough to want the credit for every bit of me.

Boyfriend

"I don't want to see other people" he announced after our third date. *"I want to see you exclusively".*

"Does this mean you are my boyfriend?" I asked.

"Boyfriend?"

He cringed.

When this dialogue took place I had been out of the dating scene for a bit. 20 years, to be exact. The world had become a different place and I found myself unequipped to interpret a whole new landmine-strewn nomenclature. An overwhelming amount of subtleties and implications were going over my head. I realized, a bit too late, that certain words I had always known were now loaded, and therefore off limits. Apparently, "boyfriend" was one of them.

To be clear, I was not treading anywhere near the even more incomprehensible realm of (gasp) relationship definition. Nothing even close to *"where is this going? What do I mean to you? Before we go any further, will you love me forever?"*

This was more about a dilemma about vocabulary.

How am I supposed to refer to a person of the opposite sex whom I am not married to but who is, well, "special"? (I was going to say "mine", but I now know better.)

And what do I call him now that we are living together but are not engaged or married?

I could refer to him as "my dude", but I'm not that hipster. I find both "admirer" and "suitor" to be presumptuous and one-sided. "Betrothed"sounds too royal. "Beau" does have a *je ne sais quoi*, but isn't homey. "Confidant" holds too many secrets. "Escort"sounds like I would need to look into service renewal. "Flame" is hot, but flickering. "Fellow" is affectionate, yet too casual. I could call him my "friend", which he is, or my "companion", which is technically accurate, but then, for the sake of precision, I'd have to mention the additional benefits our friendship comes with, which you'd rightfully consider TMI.

"Significant other" is stiff. "Lover" is too one-faceted, as is "object".

I could call him "cutsicle"; according to the urban dictionary it's the word to use "when someone is so cute you can't handle their cuteness" which certainly applies but doesn't really suit his personality.

Tragically, this is also the case with "stud muffin".

I could call him my "boo", but when I tried it out he rolled his eyes. Or "bae", except I can't really pull that off. I'm not even sure exactly how to pronounce it.

I could go for "fiancée", but that would be misleading. "Partner" sounds like we work in a law firm or should be on horses and "roommate" leaves out one of my favorite parts, the one that hints at romantic entanglement and other shenanigans.

As exuberant as I tend to be, I did feel "knight" would be too melodramatic.

After weighing all my options I decided that referring to him as Boyfriend gives him a solid title that clearly explains what he is in reference to me, is both socially appropriate and universally understood.

As an added bonus, Boyfriend subtly honors the fact that he makes me feel like a teenager, in an exciting, adventurous, I-really-wasn't-expecting-this-to-happen-to-my-life-and-thank-you-for-being-so-wonderful sort of a way. It's committed, yet fun. Exclusive, without being excessively possessive. Young, which we both are. Sort of.

I'm going with it.

Filthy Rich

At the risk of sounding excessively extravagant, here are some things that most convey opulent wealth to me:

Going to the doctor for a check up and hearing him confirm you have a clean bill of health.

Looking in the mirror and realizing that you may not be perfect but that you are pretty damn beautiful.

Throwing a birthday party and finding yourself in a room full of good friends.

Being in regular contact with a loving family.

Getting paid well to do something you love.

Ending the day by putting your feet up against the feet of someone snuggly (this "someone" could most definitely be a puppy).

Going to sleep knowing in your heart that you will always have enough.

These are all spectacular displays of a person whom I would consider to be filthy rich.

How To Love Yourself

When I was in my early teens I had a mad crush on a boy.

The subject of my love (the boy) changed pretty regularly.

What remained constant was the mad crush.

I felt like I would do anything to make him happy. I loved every little thing about him, even his quirks. I wanted to give him everything.

Until I lost interest, met another boy and began again.

The thrill and devastation of the mad crush roller coaster.

One day, in that vast, cold, gray, dry, empty expanse between one crush and another, I wondered if I had ever felt that mad love for myself.

Would I do anything to make me happy? Could I love every little thing about me, even my quirks? Would I give me anything?

I decided it was time to set aside the boy crushes and instead nurture a new kind of love. It seemed like a better investment of my time and energy to love someone I would always have by me, who would never neither bore me nor leave me.

Thus began a shift in my perspective.

I wasn't dieting because a boy wanted me to be thinner. I was eating better because I wanted to be healthy. I was taking care of myself.

If someone wasn't sure how they felt for me or wanted me to be someone I wasn't, rather than wanting to cling and desperately figure out how I could make them love me, I instead felt I deserved better.

I stopped being interested in those who weren't interested in me.

Instead of wondering how on Earth I could be good enough to deserve someone's unconditional love I became pickier about who I loved. This selectiveness did not come from a place of arrogance but from a place of self esteem.

I became more comfortable with uncertainty because I trusted I could probably figure out how to deal with whatever happened next.

I began to believe in myself, because that's what you do when you love someone.

I have learned the importance of spending time alone because I need to reduce background noise so I can listen to myself. How am I feeling? What do I need? What is it that I'm trying to tell me?

I recognize where I need help and give myself the space and the tools to bolster those areas without judgement and without being hard on myself. For example, I have a tendency towards anxiety, so I search for things that calm me (I try to go to yoga several times a week and pay attention to how I'm breathing.)

I try to be what I am looking for. I want to be loved with a love that is true and deep and stable. I want someone who will always want what is best for me. I want someone I can count on.

That's what I work on becoming for myself.

The Most Beautiful Equation

I used to believe I needed another to complete me.

My other half.

I thought the most beautiful equation was

1 + 1 = 1.

It took me years to understand that I was created whole.

How perfect is that?

The most beautiful equation to me is

1 + 1 = 2

I am complete all on my own.

Nadie Aprende En Cabeza Ajena

There is a saying in Mexico: *"Nadie aprende en cabeza ajena."*

The literal translation is: *Nobody learns in someone else's head.*

A mom might ask her son not to jump up on the furniture. *"You're going to fall"* she might say *"and it will hurt".* So the kid jumps on the furniture and slips and falls and she laments the fact that *"nobody learns in someone else's head".*

Your friend might say *"Don't date that guy. You already know he's a player".* You date him anyway and end up hurt.

You had to go out and experience it for yourself.

We often wish we could save others the trial or the pain but the truth is people learn only by making their own mistakes.

There are no shortcuts.

Strange Kid

I've heard from child psychologists and experts that children assume every family is like their own, because it's the only thing they have ever known. I don't know if that's true in general, but I do know it's not true for me.

Having grown up in Mexico in the 1970's, I always knew that other people's parents were married to each other. That other people did not have brothers and sisters from different mothers or fathers. That other people went to mass on Sundays and I went to the movies. That while other people went to summer camp or Disney World I went to Egypt, China, Italy, Greece, France and Japan.

My mother hated Walt Disney. I didn't know who Snow White was, Sleeping Beauty or Cinderella. I never assumed people lived happily ever after. I was not once even offered a bite from the poisoned apple of fairy tales.

In the stories I was told, the only girls who wore fluffy white dresses and dainty shoes were the dancers of Degas. I did not believe I needed to be kissed to wake up and I did not believe waiting for anything would be conducive to my happiness. While I never believed in Prince Charming, I did believe the image of a pipe was not a pipe because it said so.

Distinguishing between a villain and a hero was never black and white. Attila the Hun promised his brother tribe, the Magyars in

Hungary, that he would always be there for them. He said if they needed him they would hear the thunder of the hoof beats of his horses as his troops came to their rescue. *"Alive I shall cross the Earth"* he said *"and dead I will descend from the heavens".* Ruthless, maybe, but Attila kept his word to the people that he loved.

I heard more about tropical islands than enchanted castles, and yet I never really warmed up to Gauguin, who left Van Gogh when he needed him the most.

I learned that if even the Gods living in Olympus had characteristics of mortals, then it was fair to make allowances for a mortal's limitations.

In our house, there was no honor in having ruby red lips and blue eyes with long lashes. Admiration was reserved for heroes, for the man in the arena, for people who achieved against all odds, for men whose reach exceeded their grasp.

At school, after the teacher heard fourteen "How I Spent My Summer Vacation" recounts, I would talk about the 8,000 terracotta soldiers of Xian, how each of their hair styles and faces was different, how the site included terracotta camels and horses, and that I had seen them all.

By now you've probably gathered I was not the most popular kid. The funny thing is, contrary to everyone else, I did not ever feel that these differences made me strange. I assumed they made me special.

You can expect this from children, you know. Being made to feel special was the only thing I had ever known.

The Liar Within

In silence
I admonish my lack of courage

you are so afraid of everything
so small
you don't know what you are doing
this is the end of the line

then you ask if I am happy
if I know who I am
I open my mouth
to confess
to let it out
but find it impossible to say this aloud
it would not ring true

There is a liar in me and I will beat her every morning

The Best Of Ourselves

I am an introvert.

My life is highly social.

All day I scatter precious energy and invariably come home completely depleted, craving a dark corner to hide in.

I often notice that I give all my energy away to people who are less important to me than Boyfriend and then come home with little left for him.

The things that matter the most to me and where I spend the bulk of my time don't always match up.

Are we giving strangers the best of ourselves and leaving whatever is left over for those we love the most?

If so, shouldn't we be making some changes?

Superpower

Right in front of the store there was a group of five young men. They were noisy, rowdy, jostling, joking.

A young, pretty woman walked past them and they whistled, teased and briefly blocked her path so she had to walk around them.

I watched all this from a short distance and dreaded the fact that I needed to go to the store too.

I took a deep breath and started walking.

Do you know what happened next?

Nothing.

They didn't notice me.

Have you ever felt invisible? A lot of women feel this way when they go from young to middle aged.

It's disconcerting to suddenly feel others don't know you are there.

As I was getting used to this I realized I could listen to people's conversations. I could see things I couldn't before: I had a much better, clearer view of human nature.

Invisibility is a superpower.

Your Memory

As hard as I've tried it's impossible for me to pinpoint when my father's cognitive decline began.

The initial symptoms of his dementia seemed like an exacerbation of his personality. It eventually became clear that he was losing his short-term memory.

The first thing to go was his ability to work. He lacked the focus necessary for the most basic follow through. He could not keep appointments straight.

In a professional sense, after a life of power and influence he became useless.

He lost his patience. He couldn't find things. He didn't know where anything was. His glasses. His wallet. The bank. The store.

He lost his friends. How do you remain close to someone who does not show up when he says he will, who forgets everything you tell him, who keeps asking the same questions, who seems to never pay attention?

He lost his relationships. My father was a womanizer. Nothing will make a complex love life unravel quicker than an inability to keep your stories straight.

He couldn't write. He couldn't read. I could hear him pacing straight through the night. Ambition, diminished, gave way to restlessness.

He lost every scrap of inner peace.

Chaos set in. Memory is order. Without it there is no sequence of events. It's not that geographically he was confused about where he was. He also did not know where he was in the arch of time.

He dreamed all his life of having grandchildren. His son had a beautiful daughter and he could never remember her name.

Look at your children. Can you love someone if you don't remember them? Look at your wife. Can you trust someone if you have no recollection of any of the incidents that built that trust?

What about your word? Can you deliver on promises you don't remember making?

What about your authority? Can you direct someone else if you don't know what to do?

What about your health? What would happen to it if you can't look after yourself?

We knew Christmas 2013 would be his last.

I was walking in the garden and saw him through the window. Instead of heavy hearted he looked happy, surveying decorations and gifts. He caught me looking at him and waved. The reflection makes him look like an apparition.

I remember him angry and sick and scared and frustrated.

I remember the glint in his eye and the tailor made clothes and that swell of love I feel come towards me as if he was still right here.

I loved him just the same.

Memory is a lot more than our history. It's our identity.

Very Not Perfect

I have a storm of curly hair. I'm not a staggering beauty but I have what I guess you could call a presence. I like who I am, flaws, quirks, temperament and all.

When I meet someone I do so as they are. No fixing. No tailoring. No redesigning.

So when he said *"you would look so sexy with straight hair!"* I knew there was a pretty, straight-haired girl out there who'd be perfect for him.

Because thankfully, there is nothing perfect about me.

Maybe She Really Is Into You

I got a divorce a few years ago and after living alone for some time I decided I needed to try out online dating.

My motivation, more than "falling in love", was to create a new social circle.

After 15 years of marriage, your ex tends to know everyone you know and meeting new people is the only way to truly start over.

I had not dated in more than 20 years.

I cannot tell you how terrifying it was to get back out there after so long. I felt incredibly vulnerable.

I made sure that the dates I went on were early in the evening and in public places. I always let a friend know where I was going, who I was going with and what time I got home.

One night I met someone I really liked. Our date went on for so much longer than usual. At the end we stood on the sidewalk and he kindly offered me a ride home.

I told him I wasn't ready to get into a car with a stranger, and that I didn't want him to know where I lived.

I think he thought I was out of my mind.

He then asked for my phone number.

I told him he could always contact me through the dating site.

He stood there looking at me, perplexed. I had just told him I didn't trust him to take me home and had just refused to give him my number.

I so respect what he did next.

"Hey" he said. *"I had a lot of fun tonight. Did you have fun?"*

"Yes" I replied. *"A lot of fun. I'm going to get a cab."'*

"Great" he said. *"Are you interested in seeing me again?"*

"Yes" I said.

Then I drove off.

When I got home 20 minutes later I had a message from him waiting for me. We set a new date right away. (I did a little dance around my apartment.)

We have been together four years now and have been living together for two.

I am so very grateful to him for waiting for me to feel safe.

This is not a process he could have forced.

After what I did he could have concluded I was not interested. Instead, he asked.

People have complicated reasons to do the things they do, reasons that have nothing to do with you.

And they are often worth the extra effort.

Lunch Alone

I usually have lunch alone, despite the *"never have lunch alone"* maxim.

Quiet is scarce. I cherish stepping out of work, picking a café and focusing on the food before me instead of my noisy brain.

The guaranteed rush of gratitude — for how beautiful everything looks on my plate and the precious hour of peace — confirms that *"never have lunch alone"* works for many people, but it doesn't work for me.

Before My Eyes

I was flying from Los Angeles to San Francisco.

The storm was so bad the plane couldn't land. It tried to — for more than two hours it tried to, while passengers whimpered, gasped, prayed, heaved into their air sickness bags. I was sitting next to a small boy. He looked over at me and put his hand in mine. It felt fragile and cold, like a bird. I noticed my skin, dry and taught over my knuckles.

Everyone tells me I look exactly like my father, but my hands are my mother's hands. Hers are bigger, stronger, but I can see how mine were made using hers as a model. I see her in other places too — in my back and shoulders. I know I'm the spitting image of my father, but I'm my mother's daughter too.

My parents love me. Today, years later, while I pick fruit at the supermarket or slide something into the oven or straighten out my desk at the office I am often struck by this knowledge that comes out of nowhere and envelops me completely.

There was a boy I liked in school, right at the time when girls liked boys and boys thought girls were gross. He had black hair and green eyes and wore heavy metal T-shirts. In the search for something to talk to him about I introduced myself to what is now referred to as classic rock. My preference for rock outlived my interest in the boy.

When I lived in Beijing I had a dear friend who was a DJ. He used to play whatever song my friend Mimi and I wanted, and we stayed out as late as my father would let me (which was never very late) dancing with abandon in a nearly empty disco in China in 1988.

Right away I loved going to work. The structure of it, its demands on one's character. I love getting up in the morning and walking outside in my pajamas to get the newspaper, the smell of the clean ocean air. I love glancing over the business section over my breakfast of toast and blueberries. I love showering and getting dressed and showing up and getting paid for something I love doing, which mostly involves expressing my opinion. I look at my paycheck and think, *"Ha! What a deal".*

On the plane, with the pilot trying to land in the middle of that storm, I looked down at the San Francisco Bay and worried that the water would be really cold. I wondered if I'd manage to get out of my seat belt. If the cushion could really be used as a flotation device.

It's true what they say, that when you feel death is close your life flashes before your eyes.

World Champion

I had a 4 year old friend over one Sunday afternoon.

His mom says to him *"say goodbye and thank Dushka for playing with you!"*

The kid looks at me rather reluctantly. *"Thank you, Dushka".*

Then he stands there and adds *"You are the best pillow fort builder in all the world."*

And that, folks, might be one of my favorite compliments ever.

Stay

I know what you think
settled
happy
lucky
I can't deny it
so lucky

but the emptiness
it's still here
I'm scrambling
bewildered at least once an hour
unrecognizable to myself
old

strong
precious
some day obliterated
gone without a trace

too much
suffocates me
not enough
never enough

a perpetual desperate search for my better self

I don't know how to keep her here

Diamond

Boyfriend is meeting my dad for the first time. They're drinking from a bottle of Japanese Whiskey Boyfriend purveyed for the occasion.

Boyfriend: *"What was it like to raise four kids?"*

Dad: *"They get sick and argue and don't come home when they say they will and you worry constantly. It's not for the faint of heart."*

Boyfriend: *"Tell me about Dushka. What was she like?"*

"Boyfriend." My Dad says, eyes shining. *"Dushka was perfect".*

My Dad died 8 months ago today. While the world reminds me daily of my flaws and shortcomings, this is the diamond — resplendent, indestructible — my father left lodged in the center of my heart.

My Soft Blanket

It's quite possible I am the toughest person to find a gift for.

I don't like jewelry. I don't wear make-up. I have an aversion to clutter, don't like stuff, and consider editing my closet way more fun than shopping.

To top it all off, if there is ever anything I feel like getting I buy it for myself.

One day over a year ago Boyfriend and I were walking around San Francisco and a blanket caught my eye.

I have a THING for texture. I LOVE SOFT THINGS.

Mmmm.

This blanket was very very soft. I stood there petting it. Then I put it down.

Boyfriend, who happens to be quite the shopper, tried to convince me to buy it but I did what I always do when I go shopping: I decided I didn't need it.

Over the course of the following months I mentioned the blanket a few times. (It was so soft...)

Boyfriend would look at me reproachfully. (I mean, he did advise me to get it.)

On our three year anniversary he came home with a box.

"I told you not to get me anything! Why? Why? Why? Why did you?"

Inside, wrapped in crisp creamy tissue paper, was my very soft blanket.

I love it so much. If I'm home, the blanket and I are one. I curl up with it and write. I curl up with it and read. I curl up with it and look out the window.

Revolutionary Blood

Emiliano Zapata was a hero of the Mexican Revolution.

When my mom first met my dad she asked if he was related.

My dad, being very young and wanting desperately to impress a beautiful woman, said yes.

My mom believed him.

If it wasn't for the fact my dad made up a story about having revolutionary blood, I might not exist.

Best Case Scenario

I will immediately, unfailingly go to the worst possible case scenario.

It's not that I'm a pessimist. I'm an optimist who concluded long ago that to accurately assess a situation I needed to ask *"what's the worst that could happen?"* The assumption is that if I have evaluated the worst, I will be ready for anything.

I have discovered that this is flawed reasoning, because:

It's impossible to prepare for *anything*, given that the combinations of unfortunate things that can happen are, I'm sorry to say, infinite. So, when something bad does happen, rather than being "ready" I sit there bleary eyed and wild-haired wondering how on Earth I did not see it coming.

Operating in worst case scenario mode leads me to live in a perpetual state of heightened anxiety. (It's no wonder, since I inhabit a nightmarish kind of place)

The lethally ironic blow? The exercise completely dulls my instincts, so that when something happens I cannot read my most trusty tool (my internal compass) because I've dulled it with a flood of possible scenarios that do not take place.

Ultimately, what I end up without is faith. Because I'm so busy looking ahead at likely disasters that I fail to notice all of the times that what I was expecting did not occur.

So I'm now in the middle of the most difficult exercise: training every day to resist taking my well tread, completely cleared away path that leads to worst case scenarios; and instead choosing to open through dense jungle the trail that no one has ever set foot on of trying to conceive the best that could happen.

Saying this doesn't come naturally to me would be an understatement. It scares me, because it feels like I an setting myself up to be ambushed, hurt or disappointed.

But instead of living through the heartbreak of all the catastrophes that have only happened in my (hyperactive) imagination, I hope to live through the joy of a thousand perfect (and equally plausible) outcomes.

This way, when crisis strikes, at least I won't be exhausted.

What Are You Reading?

When I was growing up we would all get together as a family for lunch on Sundays.

My father got married and divorced often and had children from different wives and vehemently claimed that *"If I don't have any half-children, no one here has any half-siblings."* We were all very close and still are decades later.

When we came to the table we were rowdy and restless and holding side chats. My father wanted the whole table focused on a single conversation. He would start every meal the same way.

"What book are you reading?"

Sometimes we went around the table but most of the time one answer led to questions or commentary and kept everyone focused on the same theme throughout the meal.

My Dad died almost a year ago. I miss him desperately. My siblings and I talk on the phone several times a week and I always know what everyone is reading.

Bring It On

We believe we can escape fear by avoiding the circumstances that cause it.

If we are afraid of flying we can resolve not to travel by plane.

If we are afraid of being hurt we can close off our heart.

The truth is the more we adapt our behavior to fear, the more we give it power, and the more it grows.

We cannot let fear make our decisions, because that means it will take over our life.

Adolescent Vigor

There was a boy I liked in school, right at the time when girls liked boys and boys thought girls were gross.

He always sat in the back row, doodling. He almost never spoke. Black heavy metal T-shirts were like his uniform.

I loved him.

In a frantic search for something to talk to him about I introduced myself to what is now referred to as classic rock.

My preference for rock outlived my interest in the boy.

Then there was the boy who stood outside my school waiting for his friends. I could see from across the street that his eyes were blue.

And the boy who called my brother, back when homes had one land line we all fought over. I answered the call and we ended up talking for hours. He called me every night for months but we never met.

I wonder if my brother ever knew.

There was the man siting in the corner at a bar in Paris who I never saw again and the one sitting next to me on the plane on a flight to New York that I never exchanged a word with.

When I lived in Beijing my friend Mimi and I stayed out as late as my father would let me (not very late), dancing with abandon in a nearly empty disco in China in 1988. I fell in love with the DJ. To this day I am convinced he sent me secret messages through the music he chose to play. *("I just want your extra time and your kiss".)*

Once, at a work related meeting, I saw a man give a presentation about a tech launch. I was supposed to be learning about global strategy but what I was really thinking, with a giddy, somewhat sick feeling, was *"I love him"*. Later that day someone introduced us and I told him I liked his tie. I married him shortly after.

When Boyfriend and I were on our third date we spoke — in careful, logical, abstract terms — about love. He explained that "love" was a big, serious word, never to be used lightly. To my untrained ears it sounded like a plot to walk barefoot through shards of glass.

I paid close attention to what he said, and intellectually a part of me agrees. But I have come to accept that my heart does what she does. She loves. Despite her adolescent vigor, utter absence of outlook and possibly calamitous nature, I like her this way.

Loving instantly and often has proven to be a grand way to go through life.

Intolerance

My life goes something like this:

Me: *"Hi! Breakfast veggie burrito please. No tomato - I'm allergic."*

Him: *"WHAT? Tomato is so good for you!"*

Me: *"Yes, unless it's toxic to your system."*

Him: *"Well, we can put a little in, just for flavor."*

Me: *"No - but thank you!"*

Him: *"Oooooh. Ok. Well, how about sun dried tomato?"*

Me: *"Thank you! But, that won't work."*

Him: *"But it's sooooo delicious! I just can't imagine what it would be like!"*

Me: *"It's hard. Sometimes very hard."*

Him: *"A little pico de gallo on the side?"*

Me: *"That's chopped up tomato, so no."*

Him: *"Wow. You know, I just don't get it."*

No kidding.

Naive

I might have been the only one
who believed all of it

you and me
like blood

our lives intertwined forever

we were instead inane
prone to rapid disintegration
in the place of a broken memory

carefully preserved
painful
precious

there is nothing
a nuisance

a hairline fracture on a crystal pitcher
dirty dishes piled in the kitchen sink

I used to think
what a waste loving you turned out to be

until I realized

everything I know now
about being happy

I learned from you

Advice

My dad was the king of making bad advice sound like it made good sense.

When I got married the first time he was on marriage number three. I was experiencing a bad case of cold feet.

"Sweetheart." he said. *"Just marry him. It's not as if it was forever".*

Balance

I have an aversion to one-size-fits-all buzzwords that we are expected to strive for.

If we are all different, how could the same concept be right for everyone?

Let's talk about this unrealistic objective we call "balance".

Roosevelt encourages us *"to know the great enthusiasms, the great devotions"* to *"spend ourselves in a worthy cause"*.

"Something is always born of excess" said Anais Nin. *"Great art was born of great terrors, great loneliness, great inhibitions"*.

"Do not go gentle into that good night" warns Dylan Thomas in one of the best lines ever written. *"Rage, rage against the dying of the light"*.

My favorite parts of life — irrational optimism, falling in love, conviction, feeling captivated, elated, inspired, impassioned — are unbalancing.

Balance is not all it's reputed to be.

More to my initial point, balance is not who I am. It's in my nature to be "all in"; to be completely absorbed by what interests me.

I see the world in black and white — a middle ground just does not occur to me. I take sides. I don't dabble. I dive.

I find an absolute much easier than moderation. I'm not saying this is right, or that I recommend others be this way. I'm saying it's who I am.

If you set a plate of still warm, crunchy chocolate chunk cookies on the table I have zero problem saying *"No, thank you"*. But if I have a cookie, I will want another.

I have discovered that for me the key to discipline and good health is abstinence, not moderation, even though moderation is often forced upon me. *("Come on Dushka! Relax! Live a little! Have just one teeny slice!"* You don't understand. One teeny slice is not how my brain works.)

I have found tremendous solace and power in accepting who I am. I will always want to be better, but I will not want to be someone else.

I'm sure balance is a golden goal for many people. But it doesn't work for me.

Pleasures

Being right in the middle of a book so good that my real life fades away for a few hours.

A nap. (Maybe after putting down aforementioned good book.)

Learning something new.

Going through something difficult, frustrating or annoying and coming out on the other side knowing I handled it with grace.

A job well done, even when it was easy.

How fresh everything looks when I travel.

A night of deep, uninterrupted sleep.

That feeling of stepping back and looking at my life as if it was a movie and I am the spectator and realizing the movie is actually really good.

Alcohol

I don't like alcohol. It makes me feel first unfocused, then woozy, then run down. It chops up my sleep. I wake up exhausted. I love working out and even a single drink the night before turns a graceful early morning yoga class into an hour where I crawl around in agony.

As if this wasn't enough, a drink has zero redeeming qualities from a nutritional standpoint. It's the poster child for the term "empty calories".

Finally, a drink or two can easily be more fattening than dessert.

I mean, give me sparkling water and give me pie.

Suspension Of Time

I have a lot on my mind.

When I have a lot on my mind, I get on the bus and stay on it until the end of the line, then get out and ride it all the way back.

Because being in transit gives me the illusion of a suspension of time.

While on the bus, I find solace in its uneven movement. I look out into the San Francisco night and its soft glimmer and am reminded just how restorative, how indispensable beauty is.

I eavesdrop on conversations, which tend to cast my own bright life in a different, more forgiving speckled light.

I glance at my phone and think, think and work in an ambulatory setting with an ever-changing view where I am not interrupted. The resulting, partially accidental productivity settles me.

I am weary of platitudes. I don't need reminders of the value of life or the importance of love or our lack of control or how change must be embraced ugh blah blah blah I already know. I know.

I don't have to be anyone here. My role in this bus is that of an anonymous, probably disheveled, mathematically middle-aged woman.

I am no one's friend, no one's coworker or lover or daughter or sister or tenant. I need to do nothing here. I am no one here, just the weak, see-through reflection on someone's large, dark window pane; the high pitched, possibly grating, foreign language phone conversation another overhears, perhaps casting his own life in a different light.

And I have the most beautiful city in the world displaying itself to me, and it's just a bit beyond my reach because really I am somewhere else right now. Somewhere that exists only in the person I used to be.

Alien Concept

I frequent a gym brimming with beautiful people.

I'm always stunned when I hear gorgeous women looking at their naked reflections complaining about what they see.

I'm deeply grateful to my mom for being so comfortable with herself that I never heard her utter such words.

For making the concept of not liking what I look like so alien to me.

I think this starts with acceptance. With loving not just what our body looks like but the miracles it can do.

But then instilling in our daughters the truth about their inherent beauty.

Inner Circle

We were friends. Good friends. Until she came over to me at a party and accused me of horrible things.

I listened at first, then asked her to stop. But she wouldn't stop. That's when I realized she was deriving pleasure from the fact that she was hurting me.

I cried that night. Not over what she said. Over the disbelief of having witnessed my friend become somebody else. Someone I didn't know. A stranger. A foe.

She sent a long email late the next day. She explained that nothing of what she said had anything to do with me. She was going through things, she wrote, and inexplicably took it out on someone she knew would not counterattack. She apologized.

I forgave her. I tried to get things back to the way they were. But I could not.

The people you let in close, your inner circle, are those who support you, who want what's best for you. Not aggressors. Not people who enjoy your discomfort.

"Frenemy" is not a word.

It's entirely possible for a friend to disagree with me or tell me I am dead wrong. But this can, without exception, be delivered free of cruelty.

You teach people how to treat you, and I don't want to have to be wary of my friends. From my friends what I want is love.

Nothing between us was ever the same.

I still miss her sometimes.

Trust is a delicate thing.

Home by 9:00

When I was 16 I had a strict, conservative Dad who imposed regular curfews. Mostly I acquiesced but sometimes I'd try out some sass.

Him: *"I want you home at 11:00 p.m."*

Me: *"But -"*

Him: *"Home at 10:30."*

Me: *"Hey! I just -"*

Him: *"Be home at 10:00."*

Me: (Certain I would floor him) *"Why? I could have sex during the day too, you know."*

Him: (Not even looking up from his book) *"I'm not concerned with your virginity. I'm concerned with your safety. Home by 9:00."*

Sass never was very effective.

Amit

I met Amit over 15 years ago at a party.

I overheard the word "soccer" and my then husband was looking for a soccer team to play on so I introduced them.

Since that day, Amit has been a fixture in my life.

Amit and my ex played soccer every Sunday, but Amit made it a point to call me and ask me how I was doing at least once a week. To my astonishment, he wasn't asking as a formality. He actually wanted to know.

As luck would have it, I ended up divorcing Amit's soccer buddy. I assumed I'd see a lot less of Amit, because in these situations you learn to expect collateral damage.

When it came time for Amit to ask me how I was doing, I told him the hardest part was opening my eyes in the morning. The full weight of the day hits you hard when you're going through a hard time.

For the first six months I was living alone he called me every day at 6:45 a.m. just to kick off my day. He was so punctual that I stopped setting my alarm.

Preparing food for one seemed so difficult and pointless. When Amit noticed I had no food in the fridge (did I mention that depression affects your appetite?) he made it a habit to call me from the supermarket. He'd drop off a bag of groceries on his way home.

Today, Amit's fiancé, my boyfriend, Amit and I hang out regularly. It's invariably happy, pleasant, easy company.

Amit is the most extroverted person I know and I am an introvert so when I tell him I can't see him because I need to be alone he nods wisely.

I don't know what I did to deserve him. But when someone says "friend" I see his face right away.

Closet Yogi

Boyfriend and I are sitting on the sofa.

He's contemplating breakfast. I'm contemplating life.

Him: *"Are you hungry? What would you like?"*

Me: *"Sometimes I feel like nothing is in its place."*

Him: *"Have you considered that maybe everything is in its place?"*

Me: *"— ."*

Him: *"I'll scramble some eggs."*

Boyfriend. Closet yogi.

Losing Joy

Joy was the dog of my life. She was a mutt, maybe part bull terrier; absolutely beautiful, lion colored, with a strong white chest and white snout. She used to sit at my feet while I wrote or did my homework, and would sneak her way into the bed — under the covers, with her head on the pillow — whenever I let her. When I didn't, she'd lie outside my window, with her face against mine on the opposite side of the glass pane.

My mom and I (and whoever wanted to join in) used to take Joy on walks to the Ajusco, a wooded area near where we lived in Mexico City. Seeing that dog run filled my heart. She'd get crazy with joy (hence the name), and was impossible to tire.

One day, as we were walking along our usual trail, Joy heard a cowbell in the distance and took off. She ran until we couldn't see her anymore. This despite the fact we called her, whistled at her, clapped our hands at her, screamed at her, and tried to run after her.

We lost her.

We looked for her for eight hours, calling her name until we were hoarse. We walked up and down every hill, every mountain, followed every path. At one point, my mom finally said out loud what I knew to be inevitable.

"We have to go."

She looked to see how I would react, and then added "It's getting dark, and we have no food, no water and no flashlights."

Then, to make me feel better "We'll come back tomorrow."

I turned around towards the parking lot and cried. I got in the car and cried (I want to cry now, more than 15 years later). I cried all the way home. I drank a tall glass of water, turned down dinner, and took a hot shower. My mom came down to my room. "We'll get up early," she said "and we'll get back there and we'll find her".

"Mom" I said. "We'll never find her. We looked everywhere today. She's gone, mom."

I got no sleep that night. I tossed, and all night Joy's new friend Cool cried. Not the weak whimper of the restless puppy that he was, but desperate, heart wrenching howls of a grown wolf in agony. Long, drawn out "aoooooo, aooooo" pierced the night. You have never heard an animal so upset. We worried Joy's disappearance would kill him (I worried it would kill me).

As soon as the sun came up, we met up in the garage. We got into the car without saying a word. I felt sick. I knew she'd starve, or that someone would hurt her. Even in the best of circumstances, she'd be so confused — who else would give her the kind of a life we gave her?

Meanwhile, my mom was really chatty. She had a plan. She had thought about it all night. I was only half listening.

"We have to think like a dog," she was saying. "Think like a dog. Think. Like. A. Dog. If you were a dog, where would you go? I think we'll find her in our picnic place. It's a spot she associates with food, and she'll be hungry."

Gone, I was thinking. Gone, gone, gone.

We trudged up through the hills, hollering her name. I looked down ravines, imagining finding her body. How can a domesticated, good-natured, big-hearted, honey eyed dog survive a whole night of freezing temperatures, lost in the wild? How can Joy, who likes to sleep with her head on a pillow, for goodness' sakes —

That's when I heard the soft, rattling sound of her leash.

I looked ahead. And saw her. And screaming her name — startling her — ran towards her. She looked at me. Our eyes locked. Mine said "OH MY GOD ARE YOU ALRIGHT OH MY GOD OH MY GOD?" Hers said "Oh, wassup?"

She wasn't panting, or dirty, or matted, or skinnier, or bloody, or in any way showing she had just survived a terrifying night. She was like "Whatever. That was kind of fun. Anyone got anything to drink around here?"

I hugged her thick neck, and scratched her belly, and took in the woodsy smell of her paws. I ruffled her head, held back her ears, and kissed her cool, wet nose. Without turning, she rolled her eyes and turned them towards my mom with a look that said "Jeez. What's gotten into her?"

I could barely see through my tears. I dried my eyes and nose with my sleeves, and made an effort to compose myself. Hugged her again. Leashed her. Checked the collar to make sure she wouldn't get away again. Stood up and looked around, squinting at the light.

We were at our picnic place.

Color

Most of my clothes were gray. Sometimes brown. Ever so often I'd make a conscious effort to buy something with color, and it would end up at the back of my closet, incongruous and forgotten, a dot of pink standing out in a colorless ocean.

The walls of my house were all linen white. I liked very much to sit in a room and look through the frame of the door into the other at the crisp, clean lines of white on white.

One restless night I got out of bed knowing I had to paint the walls. I walked through my house taking notes, picked the surfaces that needed color and settled on four hues: red, green, blue and yellow.

Headed back to bed, I passed by my closet and was startled by what has obviously been happening for years: splotches of green, red, pink, blue, yellow; and a bit of gray, incongruous and forgotten in an ocean of color.

The Place I'm From

Oh Mexico City.

I owe you so much and I owe you nothing. I love you and despise you and you frustrate and captivate me.

I swear you off and I keep coming back and look out the window of the plane when I leave and feel desolation in my heart and cry.

You are by far my unhealthiest relationship.

No Threat

I have a boyfriend. I love him very much.

I am not remotely interested in other men.

Yet I find many, many other men attractive.

I am drawn to competence and my work exposes me to oodles of highly competent people.

I came generously equipped with an impressionable heart that is easily fascinated.

The feeling of my heart skipping a beat makes me happy.

I think finding another attractive, far from "wrong", is life affirming and a gift.

The gap between my heart skipping a beat and this coming anywhere close to threatening my relationship is about as wide as The Milky Way.

Sometimes Boyfriend finds someone attractive and I feel a smidgen of jealousy.

I then decide he should also bask in this life affirming gift; and that it stands to reason he too feels this gap, certain and true and as wide as the Milky Way.

When You're Ready

My house it reminds me
Some day I will sit on the Adondirack chair in the backyard
Learn how to use a tagine
Read all the books on my bookshelf
In alphabetical order
Lie in the wide red sofa or on the cool wood floor
And watch the moon through the skylight
Wear my sequined T-shirt and all those boots
Use the hot tub burn candles
Apply beauty treatments
I'll learn to knit
Take in every single photograph in the coffee table books
Sip Turkish coffee from the small white cups
Some day I'll have time for this my house assures me

You go do what you need to do and we'll be here when you're
ready

Good Humans

At Heathrow Airport I left my purse hanging from a hook in the back of the bathroom stall door.

Inside this purse: everything. Wallet, I.D., credit cards, cash, passports, phone, blackberry, boarding pass, a notebook and my planner.

I walked out of the stall, washed my hands and waltzed out of the bathroom unburdened, with a spring in my step.

About 3 minutes later I froze. My bag was not on my shoulder.

I felt panic, complete with a racing heart and sweat trickling down my stomach.

I ran back to the bathroom practically incoherent and banged on the door of the stall I had used. I stammered, yelling through the paneling.

The woman who an eternity later (less than 30 seconds) came out tried to calm me but I didn't have time to be calmed.

Another woman in the bathroom explained she had found the purse and handed it to an officer.

I had visions of the bag being destroyed (because that's what they say they will do if they find a bag "unaccompanied".)

I ran. I found a uniformed man and babbled. He frowned and escorted me to a room. The room was full of abandoned bags and suitcases.

There was mine, crouching in a corner, cold and alone in a world it didn't understand. (OK. It's inert. But stay with me.) I pointed to it with a trembling finger.

The officer grabbed it and put it in my hands. He asked me to list what was inside. I did. He handed it over.

"Oh my God" I said, exultant, shaky, grateful, relieved. *"I could kiss you right now".*

"Please don't" he replied.

The Battle Within

Me: *"Some days are good. Some days aren't. Once and for all, I'd like to end the single most tortuous battle within me: the discrepancy between what I feel and what I should feel."*

Boyfriend: *"Example?"*

Me: *"Why do I still feel anxious about things I can't control? Why can't I always summon grace when I feel wronged? Why can't I replenish faith at will? Why can someone hurt me when I should be beyond their reach? Why do I worry if worry is pointless? Why do I feel an incandescent flare of rage when my heart should only harbor love? Why don't emotions have reins, like domesticated wild horses?"*

Boyfriend: *"Welcome to being human. Go get ready. You're going to be late for work."*

Boyfriend. Not a morning person.

Useless

It's not that we didn't want kids. We did, just *not right now.*

A year of "not right now" quickly (oh my god so quickly) turned into two, six, ten.
We couldn't keep putting it off. But we couldn't decide.

While "not right now" accurately described how we felt, neither of us could commit to the notion of a life without children.

We reasoned we would never "be ready" and decided one day to just "remove the obstacles". (Commonly referred to as "quit taking birth control").

By now I was in my late thirties, so we estimated conception would take time and that it would be somewhat equivalent to the time we needed.

I got pregnant about a year later. We dealt with this with what I can only describe as abject panic. We went to the doctor to confirm the news, and spent the next two and a half months freaking out.

At our next doctor appointment she did an ultrasound and told us our baby had no heartbeat.

This made me sad (it still does.) I wept for days. Mixed in with the shock and loss, however, I felt a gigantic wave of relief. So did my (then) husband.

About another year later we again got pregnant. This time we'd handle the news better. We'd be more grown up. We went to the doctor feeling collected, mature. You know, readier.

"Ms. Zapata" the doctor said as she ran the ultrasound wand over my belly. *"Congratulations. You guys are pregnant with twins."*

So, yeah. We spent the next two and a half months freaking out, only double. I had crippling nausea. Even the memory of how I felt ruins my appetite all these years later.

At the three month mark we went back to the doctor, who within a couple of minutes said I'd need a D&C. This was not a viable pregnancy. Neither baby had a heartbeat.

She was sorry.

Do you know what I felt? All the things you'd expect (sorrow, emptiness, loss) but also *shame*. This made no sense to me intellectually so it took months to articulate. You know what else? I felt incompetent. Inadequate. Inept.

I felt useless.

It took me a long time to talk about my miscarriages. The first time I shared this terrible, intimate thing I was speaking to a friend who had just lost her baby. We held each other.

It felt so good to unburden myself of this that I went and talked about it with another friend, then another.

Can you guess what I found to be the most common reaction to *"I've had a miscarriage?"*

It was *"Me too. That happened to me too."*

Shame is a powerful, diminishing force. It has a way of wrapping things up, encroaching them, burying them, making them heavier and heavier.

We shouldn't have to carry heavy things, not when we're

mourning. We should be able to set them down.

This is why I am sharing this with you. This is devastating to go through. It shouldn't have to be lonely too.

Again!

Whenever I'm doing something I really enjoy, I fantasize about repeating the experience.

I then realize that instead of living fully in the moment I am distracted by fervently yearning for what I am actually doing.

Sigh. Humans.

Do It Now

When I was around 22 I was dating a guy quite seriously.

I found out through a common friend he was seeing someone else.

I was so angry I couldn't breathe.

I made a few calls and managed to get the phone number of the other girl. I called her and told her he was playing both of us. I went on to say that for me, it meant that it was over. I hung up the phone.

I wish I could tell you I did this because *"I believe women should unite against men who play them."* Or that *"it's never the fault of the other woman, but rather the guy, and we need to stick together."*

But the truth is I was acting out of spite.

I felt awful about this for years. I had recurring nightmares that I ran into him in various public places. In my dreams he would always vanish right before I could get to him to apologize.

Many years later I searched for his name on Facebook. I direct messaged him saying I did not want to disrupt his life but that if he gave me permission, his phone number and a time to call, I wanted to talk to him. He replied immediately.

We had a long talk the next day. I told him straight up I was so very sorry for what I had done. He said that he thought a lot about me over the years, that I had been very important to him, and that he too was incredibly sorry for the way he had acted.

It was a beautiful call and when it ended I felt I had put down an enormous burden.

I wish the story ended here, but it didn't.

A year after our call he died in an accident, leaving behind his wife and two young children.

I know you've heard this a million times but I'm going to say it again: If you carry around something that you need to address, do it. If you have something to say to someone, say it.

We have less time than we think.

Silly

My boyfriend and I are at the playground with my niece.

She is giving us a tour of all the things she can climb on. We are asking her questions. (*"How many rungs is that? Can you climb the monkey bars? Which is your favorite game?"*)

Suddenly she turns to my boyfriend, giggling.

Her: *"You are soooooo silly!"*

Him: *"Really?"*

My niece: *"Yeah! So silly!"*

She thinks about it for a second.

"You are so silly, that on Planet Silly you would be king."

None Of My Business

When I was 15 my mom and her husband spent a lot of time with another couple. Let's call them Shelly and Sam.

One evening we ran into Sam at a restaurant. He was with another woman. They were giggling, holding hands, kissing. There was no question they were lovers.

My mom was crestfallen. I told her, *"You have to call Shelly right away!"*

"Dushka" she said. *"While this makes me sad, it's none of my business."*

I was indignant. How could my mom not tell Shelly? Wasn't that disloyal? Wasn't she a passive participant in this betrayal?

I grappled with this for many years. My mom walked on water in my eyes and I could not reconcile her decision with my opinion of her.

Twenty years later I walked into a restaurant and ran into a dear friend. In honor of a "full circle moment", let's call him Sam. He was with a lover.

Sam's wife, Shelly, was a friend.

I was in a terrible position.

Here is what I concluded:

What goes on in their relationship is none of my business.

If I tell her, I might play a role in them breaking up. This is not my place.

I have no way of knowing what their relationship rules are or what they have agreed to.

If I tell her and they break up and they patch things up later I lose them both.

What I would do is call Sam. I would say *"I want you to know that I saw you. I am very sorry that I did. I love you both very much and I hope you do right by her. I wish you both the best."*

The tragedy here is that if Shelly found out that I knew and didn't tell her she'd be angry at me, and rightly so. But it's one of those situations where there is no perfect course of action, and the one described above is, I believe, the least damaging.

You were right, mom.

Underrated

I've always had a thing for the nice guy.

The one with good friends he's known for years.

The attentive listener.

The one who makes an effort to do the right thing, even when no one would know.

The one who tells you how he feels and calls when he says he will.

The one who is compassionate and dependable, who knows what he wants and comes through for you because he loves you but also because it's who he is.

I think the nice guy is underrated.

What's Next?

A few hours before dying, my Dad was bedridden, delirious, turbulent.

"What's next?" He'd ask.

"Why don't you rest, and we will figure it out a bit later?"

"Yes," he'd say. *"I am so very tired. I need to rest."*

"What's next?" He'd say with a start 10 minutes later. *"What's next?"*

"You're tired. Why don't you take a short nap and we will take it from there?"

After hours of this, my brother walked into the room.

"What is next?"

"What is next is that you are going to die." My brother said.

My father, in the midst of severe dementia, looked right at him, and nodded.

Even when it's terrible, there is nothing like the truth.

Intruders

Dad
Mom
You, like intruders
left pieces of yourself in my heart
a long time ago

so many years later
I still come across buried relics

and dust them off
whether they are pertinent or not
to the world I live in

even if I disagree
with what they represent
I still love them

because it was you who left them there

Good Kisser

Early on (I was 15 or so) I'd see him after school. He'd be waiting for somebody else, one foot leaning against his car (well, the one he borrowed from his dad); the collar of his polo shirt sticking up.

A year or two later he seemed to always be a part of the circle of close friends of whomever I happened to be dating.

He was easy to talk to. We'd sit on the ledge of the roof of his house, legs dangling down, and smoke and speculate about the future. Would we remain friends? Move away? Would we forget each other?

While the others drank rum and coke, played poker and listened to music (now "classic rock") we'd seek out a quiet corner and sit on the rug, lean against the wall, and talk straight through the night.

"Do you think it's true" I'd ask, *"that time heals everything?"*

He'd regard me for a long while and exhale, making chains of perfect smoke circles. *"Almost everything"* he'd declare with authority. *"Almost."*

We talked about the pros and cons of the various people we were dating. Before long, anything he said seemed to have a hidden message. My interpretation: *"She's not quite right, because she's not you."*

One day right before dawn I asked him in a tone I hoped sounded disinterested and clinical if he was a good kisser. *"Well,"* he said with a cocky grin, *"I've never gotten any complaints."*

A few weeks later at a bar he was drunk and I was not and he walked towards me and I walked backwards and he walked towards me until my back was flush against an exposed brick wall. He put one hand on one side of my head and waited a full minute. He put the other on the other side. *"We're friends,"* I whispered. *"Then turn away"* he replied as he very slowly inched his face towards mine.

I didn't turn away. We ended up kissing for hours.

He called me really early the next morning. *"Are we good?"* Yes. *"Are you sure?"* Yes. *"Well, am I a good kisser?"*

"Of all the guys I've kissed" I said, *"you're a solid #2."*

We pretended we were friends for another few months before he blurted out that he loved me, had always loved me. We proceeded to have the kind of relationship one would expect from two people stumbling through their very early twenties.

I didn't know back then that every relationship tracks a path for the ones that follow so inexorable that one day you become unable to distinguish your past actions from your fate.

I didn't know then what is so obvious to me now: that nothing is more important than your friends. That the people who have known you for years become sole witnesses to a piece of you no one will ever again understand.

He was wrong, you know. Time doesn't really heal anything.

Hope

I know that impatience runs in my family.

About a year ago I was having breakfast with my dad and was surprised to find he was acting rather mellow.

Me: *"You seem mellow."*

Dad: *"I do feel more patient."*

Me: *"Teach me! What changed?"*

Dad: *"I got old."*

There is hope that our flaws can be mended.

Sort of.

Watching Over Me

The first time I ever tasted coffee was at my grandfather's house. We went to visit and the next day I woke up early and he was already up, standing alone in the kitchen. He set a big mug in front of me, poured boiling, frothy milk into it from a battered metal pot, added lots of sugar. Then, a touch of coffee, the black liquid barely staining the white. I still drink it the same way.

My grandfather died a few years ago. I didn't know him very well, but it fills me with joy to know he watches over me first thing every morning.

Indomitable, For You

When after 15 years of marriage I got a divorce I would wake up, remember where I was (not in my house but alone in an empty apartment) and begin to shake.

I'd lie there, feeling like something was crawling under my skin, and shaking.

I am an introvert and the months following my divorce have been the only time where being alone, far from providing peace or solace, felt unbearable.

I surrounded myself with people, paced around and contemplated suicide.

This is how I first learned that one could easily, so easily, die from a broken heart.

I experienced something similar — yet very different — a few years later, when I witnessed the death of my father.

I called the medical examiner, watched the men from the funeral home wrap up his body and take it away, and strode over to my room looking for the list I had made of people to notify.

On the way to my room I doubled over in pain. I am not referring to a sudden onslaught of sorrow. I am talking about *physical* pain, a pressure that went from my chest to my back and up my neck.

I thought *"I'm having a heart attack."* I considered alerting someone but decided my family had enough going on.

Besides, at the time, dying did not seem like such a terrible option.

I took an 81 milligram aspirin and faced that awful night and the days, weeks that followed.

For months after I felt the same ongoing physical symptoms: pain in my chest, a suffocating pressure, and an inability to take deep breaths.

I spoke to a doctor who suggested running cardiac and pulmonary function tests.

This is how I learned that Broken Heart Syndrome actually exists.

<u>According to The Mayo Clinic:</u>
Broken heart syndrome is a temporary heart condition that's often brought on by stressful situations, such as the death of a loved one. People with broken heart syndrome may have sudden chest pain or think they're having a heart attack. In broken heart syndrome, there's a temporary disruption of your heart's normal pumping function, while the remainder of the heart functions normally or with even more forceful contractions.

Broken heart syndrome may be caused by the heart's reaction to a surge of stress hormones. The condition may also be called takotsubo cardiomyopathy, apical ballooning syndrome or stress cardiomyopathy by doctors.

The symptoms of broken heart syndrome are treatable, and the condition usually reverses itself in about a week.

I have heard that grief recedes over time. I don't think this is entirely true. It shifts.

Initial feelings of release related to my father no longer suffering have been replaced with the ungraspable notion that I will never see him again.

But then, as it so often happens, poetry comes to the rescue, and I think of Pablo Neruda, who wrote:

"My feet will want to walk to where you are sleeping,
But I shall remain alive,
because you loved me above all else

And above all things
you wanted me indomitable."

Obvious

Boyfriend and I were recently strolling around San Francisco and I saw many posts covered with staples.

Me: *"Who on Earth walks around driving hundreds of staples into posts?"*

Boyfriend: (Staring at me incredulously) *"People post signs. Signs are removed. Staples remain."*

Me: *"OH."* (Pause). *"I wonder how many other things that are obvious to the rest of the world are not obvious to me."*

Boyfriend: *"Many. But a lot of things that are obvious to you aren't to the rest of the world."*

Drawer

With rubber bands and matchboxes
And birthday candles
Multicolored thumbtacks
And an eraser white perfectly rectangular
A black permanent marker
And coins from other countries
Paper clips
I found a key in there I plan to keep

Who knows when I'll come across something I need to figure
out how to open

Fortune Cookie

This is my favorite fortune cookie prediction ever and I carry it with me always.

"You are worrying about something that will never happen."

You see, I used to be a worrier.

I worried all the time. I worried that something was going to happen to someone I loved, or that something was going to happen to me. I worried that my family was not safe in Mexico City (where I'm from). I worried if a friend expressed anything less that ecstatic joy. I worried that I forgot to close the garage door.

Why was it hard for me to even consider letting go of something that could be making me sick?

Because, even though for a long time I couldn't articulate this, I somehow believed that if I worried about something, I could prevent it. Yup. I believed that most things I worried about wouldn't happen precisely because I worried about them. I saw my worry as a sort of protective shield, an undetectable force that swirled around the people that I loved and accompanied them wherever they went like an aura/guardian, like a halo on an angel's head.

I explained this to a friend who looked at me before asking

"Nice. How is that working for you?"

I was stumped. I was stunned.

I realized I had inadvertently been practicing being a worrier for years, and that, as such, I could unlearn it. I replaced every worry-thought with another thought. (*"All is well." "Everything is going to be ok."* Or even — *"even if that was going to happen my worry is not going to prevent it."*)

I can't say I don't worry anymore but I worry a lot less. And when I do, I get to work on letting that crap go.

My Closet

I have never considered shopping to be fun.

A few years ago I decided I would wear (slightly different versions of) the same outfit every day, setting myself free from fashion trends.

I wear a basic dress with different boots and a different sweater or wrap every day.

The reward I derive from never asking myself *"OH MY GOD WHAT AM I GOING TO WEAR"* far exceeds my interest in clothes.

My closet is simple and I wear everything in it. For trips, I never need more than a carry on.

While I love high heels, I love my feet more, so I don't own any uncomfortable shoes. (And if you tell me that high heels are comfortable, I salute your bendy, sturdy, awesome feet.)

Boots are my shoe of choice. In San Francisco, where I live, they are perfect year round.

Collective Nouns

In the hope that this delights you as much as it did me, I hereby inform you that the collective word for cats is an intrigue, a parade for elephants, a tower for giraffes, a thunder for hippopotamus and a conspiracy for lemurs. Also, a romp for otters, a crash for rhinoceroses and a murder for crows.

Now excuse me while I locate an exaltation of larks.

Our Date

Boyfriend, whom I live with, loves Scotch. He drinks it straight, pours the amber liquid into a squat, wide glass; then sits back with a satisfied grunt.

I recently learned they opened a new bar that serves only whiskey and Scotch. I thought he'd like it so I went to scope it out.

The wall behind the bar in this new place is made up of backlit glass shelves all the way to the ceiling, full of bottles and bottles of various whiskey and scotch.

I sent a note to my boyfriend:

"I'm taking you out on a date on Saturday.
Wear a jacket.
Be ready at 7:00 p.m."

At the appointed time we hopped into a cab. He tried to guess — unsuccessfully — where we were going. I looked at him impassively, betraying nothing. (*Muahahahahaha*)

We walked into the bar and he ogled the wall, impressed.

He studied the menu very carefully.

He ended up ordering a "flight" of whiskey to sample something he hadn't tried before.

I don't drink but I took a couple of tiny sips to share the experience (It made my lips feel warm and then I winced.)

We had a chance to unwind, talk about our week and discuss the merit of different drinks. Mostly I listened and nodded (I'm not qualified to talk about the merit of different drinks.)

I like learning about things I wouldn't normally be interested in through those I love.

Even after years of living together, dates are wonderful.

For The Kids

My parents split up when I was three.

For a long time they remained in touch "for the kids", except we left home over 25 years ago and they still see each other twice a week.

"I want to make sure he doesn't need anything" she tells me.

"I visit your mom" my Dad confides *"because I need to see if she is OK."*

Ambidextrous

I am right handed and broke my right arm in a car accident in my early twenties.

I was completely thrown off balance by how deeply this affected me. I felt useless and suddenly vulnerable; slowly slipping into what I now understand was depression.

(I mention this because the knowledge that we are emotionally affected by injury would have been helpful to me at the time: it wasn't just a broken arm but a collision with my sense of mortality. It was that age were you think things only happen to other people.)

Getting back to doing everything I could do before carried a sense of urgency that went beyond the functional: I felt I was drowning.

I discovered it was easier to do things with my left hand if I "trained" it with bigger things first; those that required less precision.

Before forcing it to write I tried getting dressed. Before trying to type I tried getting showered. I wrote on a large blackboard.

After a while (a few weeks) I was ambidextrous, if maybe sloppier with my left hand (my penmanship was better with my right hand but, truth be told, to this day is pretty much illegible no matter what hand I'm using.)

I was in a cast for nine months. Doing everything with my left hand changed my perspective: I felt the world operated upside down and I had never noticed.

It taught me that even though you want to understand others you don't really, unless you have walked in their shoes.

Angel

To understand what I'm about to tell you, there are a few things you need to know.

I grew up in Mexico City.

Mexico City has a near-perfect temperate climate. It's seldom below freezing and never snows.

When I was 14 there was a boy in my class who was always getting expelled.

Let's call him Angel, because believe it or not that was actually his name.

One morning at around 10:30 Angel threw open the door of the classroom. We were all at our desks, in the middle of a lesson.

From the frame of the door he flung 10 snowballs at his friend, who sat clear across the other side of the room.

I remember the noise he made when he opened the door. His cackle, so jarring against the silence inside the classroom. I remember the trajectory across the entire room of 10 perfectly shaped snowballs. I remember the teacher, slack-jawed, speechless; the look on everyone's face as we all took in what was happening.

I found out later Angel (expelled again) arrived late because he spent a good part of the morning making snow out of scraping ice cubes and figuring out how to get them to school before they melted.

I spent years wondering what would motivate someone to go through so much work to be disobedient.

Except I can now tell people that a boy I went to school with threw 10 snowballs at someone else in a classroom in Mexico City in the middle of summer.

Angel gave me my favorite classroom memory.

Like Death

I had been married 15 years to a man who is now one of my greatest friends.

We felt the relationship was missing something and wanted things to be better for both of us.

I regarded divorce like a big break-up; and felt that we were so close and such good friends we could navigate it free of pain and complications.

I don't regret divorcing him: it was the right thing to do. And we did in fact remain the closest of friends.

But divorce is not like a break up. It's more like a death.

Complications are inherent to divorce. I was right in assuming we'd navigate it successfully. We never, not even once, argued over anything legal, practical or financial, we were never underhanded or hurtful; despite of which I do feel like something inside me cannot be repaired.

I regret that I underestimated the enormity of divorce.

Outlines

I have never been to South Africa

or Madagascar
or Nebraska

never owned red soled shoes
or painted my toenails blue

have never been seriously ill

never felt the absence of my security net
one that hangs unfailingly beneath me
every time I make a difficult decision

I've never been accused of a crime
have never committed one

have never wanted to look back
even though sometimes I have to

I have never until now drawn attention
to all these things

always there
outlining me
yet previously invisible

You're Welcome

I read somewhere that when we get up in the morning we leave behind a lot of humidity in the bed from having slept in it.

It's important to pull the sheets off so that the sheets, the mattress, the duvet and the pillows all have a chance to thoroughly dry.

This can only mean one thing: a legitimate sounding reason to never again have to make your bed.

Making Myself Uncomfortable

I am an animal of habit.

I have a natural tendency towards structure and discipline.

I crave routine and rarely second guess what I have told myself I need to do.

Here is the catch:

Anytime life has whacked me out of my established routine (moving countries, moving homes, resigning from a job, taking a new job, getting a divorce) I find that I am at my most alive.

I've learned that the very routine I crave ends up dulling my senses.

The habit that has done me the most good is to make it a point to shake things up for myself when I feel I have gotten too comfortable.

Discomfort is vital for growth.

Legendary

My parents are the stuff legends are made of.

They both have very strong personalities and shared an epic ambition.

By "epic" I mean they never were interested in "a simple life", nor aimed to rise within the ranks of an organization.

Rather, they both set their sights on being written into history books.

Their relationship was fiery, intellectual, outrageous and sometimes violent.

My parents split up when I was five. This was in great part due to irreconcilable differences but also because my father was an incorrigible womanizer and my mother would have none of that.

I never in my life heard her speak ill of him.

Through the years and many subsequent wives my Dad always sustained that everything he later became he owed to my mother.

They remained close for over 50 years. They saw each other regularly, claiming it was "for the children" but their communication continued for decades after their kids had gone.

They always fought. They always frustrated each other to a froth. They always stood by each other.

My mom frequented him through 7 years of slow progressing, lethal dementia. Even as he became less of who he was, he was somehow still the person she knew.

She visited him through two harrowing years of a cancer diagnosis that ultimately took his life.

I sat with him when he died. Asking about her was one of his last questions.

Every single thing that I am I owe to my parents.

I am rarely intimidated. I know who I am. Standing my ground was vital.

I will never have a tepid life. "Good enough" does not take. I am fiercely loyal. While I don't fear confrontation I have an aversion to drama. I believe less is more. I don't attach value and meaning to stuff.

I strive ferociously to be happy.

Even if I had more than one life, I would never be able to repay my parents. I figure that all I can do is watch after my siblings (to their total exasperation) and be the very best person I can possibly be.

As if "everything" was not enough, my parents are why I write. Writing provides a deliciously familiar place: a front row seat to this beautifully unhinged, often delusional, consistently legendary thing we call life.

Pet Scorpion

"There's a scorpion on your shoulder" says a guy to another on the bus. *"I'll swat him — don't move."*

"Oh no no" he replies *"he's my pet."*

"Pet?"

"Yeah. He's not real affectionate but he's good company. I can take him everywhere."

"Doesn't he sting, man?"

"Well, he won't if I respect his space."

It takes a full ten minutes for me to realize that everything I struggle to learn about love I could learn from that man and his pet scorpion.

Rejoice In Love

Loving someone who doesn't love you back is so horribly painful it makes you wonder if life is worth living. It's from having experienced this utter despair that I would like to suggest another perspective.

It will require a leap of faith from you and a lot of work, but I think it's worth it.

Have you ever seen someone in love? Love floods us with energy. It transforms us into superheroes. It feels like we have been plugged into a higher power. I mean, we even look radiant. Being in love is such a delicious, life- affirming gift.

It also makes us feel vulnerable. We know we could get terribly hurt; so we expect this love to be returned. We want to be comfortable and safe. We want to control the situation and control others. We want a guarantee that they will feel for us what we feel for them.

But the truth is we are never really safe. We cannot control others. Alas. There are no guarantees.

If the other person doesn't love you back, it's natural to want to let your heart grow hard, to protect it from getting hurt in the future.

The thing is, you will get hurt no matter what.

The only alternative is to learn that love doesn't have to be returned.

You can rejoice in being in love no matter what the other person feels for you.

You need to, in Pema Chodron's words, *"Keep your heart soft. Keep breaking your heart"* she says *"until it opens"*.

Can you sit with all this love you feel and just hold it, reaping its benefits, taking in its energy, being infused by it, inspired by it, without wanting anything from anyone?

This is a very difficult practice that you work at through compassion, empathy, joy and meditation.

(And some days suck and nothing works and you just want to call so you can hear his voice and hang up and cry.)

I know that in the throes of heartache this is almost impossible to take in. You don't want to keep your heart soft. You want to know how to get someone else to love you.

Consider that working on yourself, no matter how hard, is more plausible than assuming you can ever change the heart of another.

Just Human

My parents.

I love them so much it makes my chest swell with gratitude.

How did I get so lucky?

The range of things my parents did and said while I was growing up is so wide it's safe to say it went from sublime to absurd, sometimes within an hour.

So often they were right. So often they were wrong. The older I get the better I understand them. The clearer I see that they were not Gods but humans. Just humans.

I can tell you one thing for sure: coming to terms with everything your parents were is so crucial to your own happiness that accepting who they were, with their beauty and their flaws, is the greatest thing you can ever do for yourself and your own relationships (which will also be flawed and beautiful.)

Don't Look Back

I never look back
After we've kissed goodbye.

You think it's because
I'm quick to move on to other things
My gait along the sidewalk strong, determined.

If you only knew.

I treasure believing you want to look at me for as long as
possible.

I am certain I feel your eyes on the back of my neck
As I walk away.

I don't turn around because I couldn't bear to be disappointed.

To twist and find instead your back to me
Your strong, determined gait far along the sidewalk
And realize that so quickly
You've moved on to other things.

The Play

My brother calls. *"I have a situation"* he says. My heart stops.

"My kids will be in the school African Play" he explains. *"My wife and I will be away due to a trip planned long ago. There will be no one there to see them."*

I pause. I am so busy at work; this would require mid-week plane travel and canceling two days full of meetings.

I tell him I cannot make it. He says he understands. We hang up.

Then it hits me. My niece and nephew are growing so fast. When will I have the fortune of another African Play emergency?

I call him back. I tell him I'm coming. I schedule the trip. I cancel my meetings. I run to the airport. I arrive the night before to read them a story and tuck them in.

The next day I am sitting in the audience so grateful that I made this decision, mostly for myself and the pleasure of seeing them (they are really adorable.) And I wonder if they will even remember, if it will matter in the long run that I'm here.

I scan the audience and see all the kids jumping and running and cavorting. Except for my nephew, who is standing still. He is looking right at me and smiling, his four year old face in an ocean of children. I will never forget the way he was looking at me.

The best thing we can do in life is to be there for the people that we love.

Inside My Head

I argue with Boyfriend in my head.

If he does something that frustrates me, I talk to him in my head first, to prepare.

I rehearse different scenarios for different ways he could react.

Sometimes this gets me all worked up.

"Hello." I say, as he walks into the house.

"Oh, hello" he replies. *"Have you been arguing with the Boyfriend in your head?"*

"No" I say. *"Of course not."*

"Would you maybe care to rephrase that?"

"Yes." I say. *"Yes I've been arguing with Boyfriend in my head".*

Real Boyfriend knows me well.

Also, he is stunningly reasonable.

Boyfriend in my head is frustrating, mostly because he is a creation I concocted from previous experiences that are not related to Real Boyfriend.

I try very hard not to argue with Boyfriend in my head. Not

because it isn't healthy but because it's an unnecessary expenditure of energy.

"You're in a tailspin again, Dushka. Take a breath" I'll say to myself.

Internal Dushka has my best interests at heart, knows where I'm coming from and is fun to talk to.

I will never stop talking to her.

High Alert

It's 1:30 a.m. and I hear gunshots.

People scream. Cars screech. *"THEY TURNED LEFT! OH MY GOD!"* Sirens. Flashing lights. Police cars. An ambulance.

I leap out of bed. Run to the window. Crouch. Pace around. Get back into bed. Fret. Toss. Turn. Try to go back to sleep, systems on high alert.

Boyfriend snores through all of it.

I get up after this bad night.

Him: *"I don't think I slept well."*

Me: *"Did the sirens disturb you?"*

Him: *"Huh?"*

Me: *"The gunshots?"*

He leaves for work skeptical; comes home that evening to report he saw the news and confirms there was a shooting the night before, right below our window.

I have never, ever seen anyone sleep with such abandon.

Just Tell Me

There it is, that inflection again.

It's imperceptible to the inexperienced ear. It would take years of training to detect the hidden strain.

But you can't fool me. I know it's there. I reach out for it, but it's like a wisp, intangible. It's gone.

"You're not worried about me, are you?" my dad says, peppy.

"Well" I say, and opt to come out with it. *"Yes, I am, as a matter of fact. Are you OK?"*

I know the answer already. I've heard it all my life.

"Of course I'm OK."

I come from a family of booming communicators. We talk. We write. We debate. We protest. When we were young and still all lived at home, we used to get together every Sunday, sit around an enormous table, and argue over a four hour meal of green salad, carne asada and chocolate cake.

Each one of us keeps secrets, though. If something breaks — and things often break — the shards of glass are quickly, efficiently swept away, lest they hurt someone.

They are everywhere, the hints, the bits, like a shattered

windshield that leaves blue glass strewn all over the highway. They leave me wondering, guessing exactly what the extent of the damage was.

Is there some perverse reason we speak in half-truths? There is not. You see, we do it to protect one another. The unspoken commandment: thou shalt not concern a beloved family member. Shhh. The children will hear.

This is why I am always suspicious. When it gets the best of me, I launch an investigation that pries, that takes days, where pieces are pasted together to form a distorted picture. Distorted because the various sources of information are caught in this perpetual dance.

Just worry me. Your silence is worse than the things you leave me to imagine.

What about me, then? If something happened that I could shield you from, would I burden you with it?

What if you heard something in my voice?

"Everything is OK." I would say. *"Peppy. Jeez. You're such a worrier."*

Dinner Time

Boyfriend: *"I'm making meatloaf."*

Me: *"I don't like meatloaf."*

Boyfriend: *"I'll also make an aioli."*

Me: *"I don't like mayo."*

Boyfriend places a plate in front of me with a thick slice of meatloaf studded with pine nuts, dried apricots, chopped olives and vegetables; it's drizzled in a homemade, warm, spicy aioli. I taste a little piece, then another, then devour it.

Boyfriend who cooks: hot.

Boyfriend who understands what feeds me: rawr.

My Watch

At first, the gun was dangling from his hand, incidental. Then, because of what I did, he pointed it at my head.

The man holding it requested my watch, and I *hesitated.*

My mom gave me this watch. She bought it for me on the first trip we ever took alone, right before I started college. We went to Paris, just the two of us. It was September. I introduced her to the Musee D'Orsay. To do it justice, we took to savoring it for a couple of hours every afternoon instead of checking it off the list after one visit.

In memory of our voyage she bought me a watch that was meant to last forever. We were at the duty free store in the airport and devoted over an hour to the search, carefully considering different models. In the end, she spent more money than she should have. Years later, I take it off only to sleep and to shower.

I look at the time and am reminded of that trip, of my mom bent over in concentration, giving the decision of what watch to get the weight of a lifetime commitment. My watch, portable proof of the inherent intensity with which my mother approaches everything.

And now I have to give it to him, and I would really rather not.

The man's hand is wrapped tightly around the grip of the gun.

His finger is on the trigger. The barrel is pushed up against my temple. I wonder if osmosis is the reason my mouth tastes like metal.

How did I come to find myself in this predicament? What is a nice girl like me doing with a gun to her head?

Let's back up a few hours.

I'm in my cubicle at work, ready to call it a day. It's around 6:30 p.m. A coworker comes by and asks if I'd like to grab a bite to eat before heading home. I know that if I do there will be a lot less traffic once I hit the road, and, I'm hungry. I say yes. We walk out of the building and a few blocks later pick a small restaurant. It has, maybe, 12 tables. We sit down. The server brings a menu. We order. The food arrives. We talk. What time is it now? Not much later than 7:30.

An odd silence, elemental, like a shudder, like cold air, comes over the room. Before I confirm the scene with my eyes, I know what this is. Everyone does.

I turn to see three men dressed in dark suits standing at the door. They are all heavily armed. One of them addresses the restaurant. He is calm, almost courteous. *"If you all behave, this will go very fast. No one needs to get hurt. We want your wallet and we want all your jewelry. Please set everything on the table."*

One of them stays by the door, blocking it. The other two pat down all male patrons. Then they go comb through the tables, systematically, putting everything into cloth bags. Unbelievably, or perhaps predictably, someone tries to make a run for it. He is quickly pinned to the floor. I think I hear the word "kill" and expect to hear a gunshot. I am grateful that I don't.

My heart is trying to thrash its way out of my chest. I am quickly putting things on my place mat. My wallet, which was gift from a friend. My ring, that I bought with my first paycheck. Small stud earrings my mother's husband gave me for my birthday. I wonder — stupidly, I know — if I can take my watch off and hide it under the cushion I am sitting on. I determine that it's not worth the risk. Farewell, watch. I feel its smooth, cool band; for the last time run my finger over the sapphire on its crown.

And you are thinking, *"how foolhardy. Does she not know that things are not important? Does she not understand she can get another watch, that the consequences of her wavering could be tragic, irreparable?"*

What am I thinking about while the barrel of the gun is resting on my temple, while the owner of the weapon is looking at me impatiently, too nonchalant to bother looking threatening?

I am thinking about you. You walk to work with a briefcase in your hand and your coffee in the other, and are not astonished by your good fortune. You go to the movies without wondering wearily if the place is going to get mugged the moment they turn off the lights. You have dinner at a restaurant and don't think twice about sitting with your back to the door. I bet you have friends who have never been held up. I bet their children play in parks outside.

Tell me, could you regard not ever feeling safe as normal?

How many times would you have to get mugged before reacting with indignity instead of terror, before you too faltered a fraction of a second too long before giving up an object you have imprudently attached meaning to?

You'd be surprised to discover what you are capable of becoming used to.

I snap off the watch and add it to the pile in front of me. The hand holding the gun to my head, showing no resentment, goes back to its dangling position, a finger carelessly threaded through the loop of the trigger. His other hand sweeps everything into the bag.

The men meet back at the entrance of the restaurant and resume their positions by the door. *"Please stay where you are. One of us might be among you, and you will get hurt if you leave the restaurant before 15 minutes are up."* They saunter off.

We all remain frozen, dried out like insects pinned behind a glass case. Long after our deadline has lapsed, we dare to stir, shake out our hands and legs. Some people start to cry. Strangers embrace. I, inexplicably euphoric, step out into this beautiful, lethal city of mine with open arms.

All Is Well

I was going through a really painful divorce and was attending yoga class as frequently as I could because it was the only part of my day where I felt a measure of peace.

I was in child's pose, barely holding on with all the turbulence I felt in my heart.

I heard the teacher say *"All is well. If it isn't, you just haven't waited long enough."*

And she was right.

Our Fragile Cornerstones

A few years ago, after exhibiting a rather odd assortment of symptoms, I went to see a doctor.

My regular medical practitioner was not available but I got a last minute appointment with her partner to get checked out.

15 minutes later I was diagnosed with a progressive, painful, long term, incurable disease that affects, among other things, your internal organs (like the heart and lungs) and is one of the leading causes of complete disability in the United States. (*"But, are you certain?"* I asked. *"Pretty much,"* he replied. *"I'm sorry."*)

The side effects of the medication prescribed to control the symptoms (such as liver damage) left me questioning if the treatment was worse than the disorder. Not taking the medication early leads to irreversible damage and deformity.

Before leaving the doctor's office I made another appointment with my regular MD to get a second opinion. Then, I took a deep dive into learning everything I could about the diagnosis.

I have always considered myself clear-headed. It didn't take long for the information I was taking in to turn me into an ineffective mass of nerves.

Have you ever felt a full-blown panic attack? Heart beating out of your chest, a thirst impossible to quench, shaky hands, burning eyes, a stress-induced fever? I felt like that every second of the following four days. I couldn't sleep more than two hours at a time. I lost half a pound a day.

I arrived a few days later for my second opinion. My regular doctor began by saying it had been inappropriate to arrive at the above conclusion without running the corresponding tests, yet conceded the symptoms I was still experiencing where consistent with the diagnosis. I went to the lab, drew three vials of blood, then had to wait 7 days to get what she said might be inconclusive results.

I left the office and did more research. When you investigate a medical condition on the Internet, there is a fine line between "information is power" (my regular modus operandi) and driving yourself crazy. I crossed it.

By Monday evening, I had not slept in four nights. Wednesday morning, I felt like death would be an optimistic outcome. This feeling was more pragmatic than depressive. The disease leaves you crippled. Which meant not only that I'd be in unbearable pain and unable to do anything for myself, but that I'd take down with me the people that I love, who'd have to take care of me. Full time. I'd had a wonderful life. Would it be worth living unable to clean myself after going to the bathroom?

A few days later I went to another doctor, a specialist in integrative medicine, because I wanted to explore every single one of my options. The gradual process of finding other alternatives (and feeling better as a result of them) gave me a spark of hope, not just in that the diagnosis might be incorrect, but that if it was accurate, I'd find my way.

I got my blood test results ten days later. They were clean. No evidence of the disease. No evidence of many others my doctor had decided to test for to *"rule out."* I cried.

For a long time I continued to have unexplained symptoms. Since then I take my health — what I eat, how I approach exercise — more seriously than ever.

It took about 5 years to feel 100% like myself.

I can't summarize all the things that went through my head when I believed my life was over.

The fatal sadness and terrifying empathy I now feel for people who are correctly diagnosed with the most terrible illnesses.

How the cornerstones of our lives are so intolerably fragile that we are conditioned to not think about it in order to make life bearable.

I'll say this much: if you have your health, everything else is solvable. Everything.

Many Lives

It's the day of my Dad's death.

He is in and out of consciousness and only sometimes knows who we are and my siblings and I are sitting around his bed, whispering, waiting.

"He did have an incredible life" my brother is saying. *"It's like he lived four lives instead of one."*

"That you know of" my dad replies.

I Like Her

It's my brain
who refers to me in the second person
an ever present stream of rebukes
like a high strung overachieving hyper conscience

you need to be better
do more
read more
try harder

despite the fact she never gives it a rest
I like the insides of my mind just the way they are

persistent noisy and architectural

Belt It Out

I love music.

I love it so much that if I hear it I need to do nothing else. At least nothing that requires that I think about anything other than the song.

I listen to music while I clean my house, while I cook, while I drive, and while I lie around listening to music.

I cannot listen to music while I write. Or work. Or carry a conversation.

If someone invites me to a party or dinner and there is background music, I cannot pay attention (to what they're saying. I pay attention to the lyrics of the song just fine.)

I have a friend who claims he listens to music while he works, but if you turn it off and ask him what he was listening to, he can't say.

He tells me he loves a song but if I ask him what it's about he doesn't know (even when he's been listening to said song for years.)

If a friend asks me to *"listen to this"* I feel the task has to be done with respect towards the request. I stop everything. I lean towards the speakers. I close my eyes.

I can relate to this compulsion to multitask, but why must we fragment pleasure? Why must we risk sensory overload?

Why not give in to the full invitation that is a good tune?

Can you listen to music while you work or while you do any other task that requires concentration? (Not me.)

If so, are you listening, or are you reducing it to white noise? Do you heed the lyrics, or just the notes? (I always know what the song is about.)

When it's a song you like, how soon after it starts do you recognize it? (Almost immediately.) How often do you know who's singing? (Almost never.)

And, if you're with me and I insist on belting out the entire lyrics, would you be irritated, or would you join in?

I hope you'd join in.

We Are Adults

When I was little all I wanted was to be big so I wouldn't have to ask for anything.

I was hyper-conscious that even small things required permission, transport and money.

There isn't a day that goes by that I don't think "I can do that! I'm a grown up! I have a credit card! I have a car!"

Being an adult is magnificent.

Antidote

To an empty refrigerator
A spacious bed
A clean floor
To having all the time in the world
To every matter I ever closed
Or gave up on
To every absolute
(Almost)
And prediction
Assumption
Preference
To habit
Ennui
Déjà vu
To independence
And carrying my own suitcase
To brittle promises
Existential questions
To nightmares
To suspicion
To forgetting
To remembering
To leaving early
To reason
Moderation
To stale dreams I forgot what box I put in

191

To sensible shoes
Gloveless hands
Pulled-back hair
To the right time and the right place
To every day feeling like Wednesday

You are the antidote

An Introvert Making Plans

Whenever we have plans, a version of the following conversation takes place:

Me: *"Oh no. I don't feel like it."*

Boyfriend: *"Let's go! It will be fun!"*

Me: *"Ugh, no. No. I don't want to."*

Boyfriend: *"Come on! You'll enjoy seeing everyone!"*

Me: *"No no no no please no."*

Boyfriend: *"OK. Would you like to stay home and I'll go?"*

Me: *"Yes. Yes! But no. I can't. We already confirmed. Why did we confirm? Why why why?"*

Boyfriend drives. I pout.

I enjoy seeing everyone.

Awe

Dedicating your life to the pursuit of awe would make for a worthwhile existence.

When I am very stressed, I feel like I can't breathe.

I relate unhappiness to feeling suffocated.

Awe to me is related to space. Breathing space.

One of the most delicious aspects of awe is that it's contagious.

People might find it in places you wouldn't think to look, but once you see it through their eyes, you feel it too.

Awe expands the heart.

What Life Has Taught Me

I was taught early on, probably in biology class, that all living things die.

I must have been around five when a bird flew right into one of the big, clear windows of my father's house. We ran to the garden to find it dead on the grass, blood on its streaked brown beak. It was still warm.

When my Dad started losing his memory, and with it chronology, logic and order (but not intelligence, which remained intact), I was in my thirties. It took me five years to say out loud that I suspected dementia.

He called me on December, 2012 to tell me he had been diagnosed with cancer. I didn't believe him. I thought it was his brain playing tricks on him.

For two years I witnessed the surgeries and the scars, the chemo and my Dad, invincible, indomitable, vain, beautiful; ruthlessly, incongruously fall apart.

Two days before he died he came banging on my door in the middle of the night. He told me, delirious, that his bed was crawling with scorpions. I walked him back to his room and held him while he slept.

He had so often done the same for me through my own

childhood nightmares.

The morning of his death he said he wanted to go to Paris, *"just you and me"*. I considered pointing out he was in no shape to even leave his room — we don't lie to each other — and instead heard myself say I'd make the travel arrangements.

He died that night.

I called the funeral home and stood there while the medical examiner confirmed his death. I watched them wrap his still warm body up in his own sheets; sat through a nine hour open casket funeral the next day, my father in a box, trapped behind a pane of glass. I kept getting hugged by people I did not recognize.

He died almost a year ago and I dream of him every night. I feel his presence all the time.
I don't actually believe he's gone anywhere.

My mother is in her mid eighties. She is a force of nature, same as she ever was, larger than life, outrageous, lucid, argumentative, indestructible.

I don't truly believe anything could possibly happen to her.

Life has taught me nothing.

Disconnect

What she wants is someone she can count on.

She dismisses the thought. She's vowed to count only on herself, to be nothing less than utterly independent. To never again be a burden on the person that she loves.

He wants to take care of her. He has to be cautious, though. Of not presuming too much, not being invasive, not transgressing on the tacit boundaries he imagines she has delineated. Of being better this time at preserving the careful balance of the life he has created for himself.

So she does things without him. It's the smallest of these she most wishes she could share. Here. Taste this, how just-right the ratio milk/coffee/sugar is. Look at the view in this rosy light. Look at the long shadows of fall.

She's standing by the window, quietly sipping from the cup he just handed her. He wonders if he finally got her coffee right. If she sees how beautiful this city that could be theirs looks in the light of early morning.

I'd like to be a part of her life, he thinks as he leaves. But she doesn't need anybody.

A Perfect Heart

I order an almond latte and look at the work of art in my cup.

"Awww, thank you! That's a perfect heart!" I tell the barista. *"I don't even want to touch it!"*

"It was made to be destroyed" he replies, impassive. *"What else is a heart good for?"*

My Father's Library

My father had a beautiful library.

Throughout my life, we'd all sit down to dinner as a family and talk and books would be pulled down from the shelves and brought to the table to prove, disprove or expand whatever we were talking about.

We all did our homework in this room and used the books as reference material.

Often, when friends came over, my father gave them a book related to the conversation we had held as a parting gift.

This beautiful room which punctuated my life no longer exists.

We recently took it down because he requested in his will that every one of his books be donated to a public library close to his heart.

Books should be loved and read and held and underlined and earmarked and referred to and given away.

Used correctly, you can never have too many books.

Jaunt

Just the other morning I discovered, possibly with disproportionate delight, that all the things I want to do more of are also my favorite words: loiter, canoodle, cavort, snuggle, frolic, saunter, shenanigans and the short, simple, counter-intuitively snappy nap.

Free Fall

My dad, who had dementia, died almost a year ago.

The last three days of his life he suffered what I can only describe as a free fall deterioration.

He came banging on my bedroom door in the middle of the night, delirious, to tell me his bed was crawling with scorpions. The very next morning he could barely make it to the bathroom. A few hours later he could not even sit up.

I will always wonder what it is that he saw on the last days of his life. He asked me that I let his mother (who died decades before) know he was on his way. (He liked things just so; so I'm glad he gave her time to prepare the premises.)

He kept trying to grasp at something right in front of him that the rest of us couldn't see.

And time seemed to run in two directions at once: he was anxious over an incident that happened long ago, and was living through one that has not yet happened (he wanted the house ready for my brother's wedding. My brother got engaged months after my father died.)

While he had a general sense of who I was, he did call me by other people's names a few times, then by the right name. He was in and out. Mostly out.

Suddenly he held my hand and looked at me. *"Thank you for being here with me, Dushka"* he said.

I took both his hands into mine and got right in his face. *"I am here"* I said loudly and clearly *"because you are the best father in the whole universe."*

He looked at me with that glint of his, his pupils focused, intelligent, so very present. *"Oh my god"* he responded. *"Oh my god."*

This conversation was the sweetest, best thing I have ever heard. It was the worst thing I have ever lived through.

Soothing Me

I can't sleep. I'm tossing and turning and Boyfriend gets up, walks around the bed and covers me with my ultra soft blanket.

Me: *"Thanks, but I'm not cold."*

Him: *"I know. But you're really into texture so it might help soothe you."*

Me: *"OK. But I've had issues sleeping for decades and there is no correlation between the - zzzzz"*

Boyfriend. Insomnia whisperer.

You Think You Know

Everything we have been taught about love is wrong.

Fairy tales teach you about princes and knights and soul mates and happily ever after.

Music drums into your brain that you can't live without another. (Wait. Or with them. Neither with you, nor without you.)

Movies depict newly anointed couples riding off into the sunset on a white Arabian horse.

This is how we believe implausible things: that our "other half" is out there. That a soul mate is something you must somehow find.

That you don't have enough air if the person you love isn't beside you.

That someone else is supposed to complete you.

That someone else can be your everything.

Nothing could be further from true love.

Love does not leave you bereft. It doesn't take who you are.

Love is not despair nor dependency.

Love is not blind.

Love sees you for who you are.

And all along we believed the poison was in the apple.

Narwhal

He came with stuff.

An antique chest, accoutrement suited for a chef, raven paintings and haiku books.

It was the narwhal whale sculpture that finally made her ask.

"Who are you? And how are you single?"

"I was waiting for you."

She nods.

It will take her some time to articulate her predicament: she believes the very things she knows aren't true.

I Want To Go Again

If I could go back in time I would want to be born to the same parents.

My father would again hold my hand in his as we stroll through the flower market.

My mother's husband would teach me how to string beads into necklaces while we sit on a shaggy white carpet.

My mother would take me to far away places every summer and gallop off into the desert on a black Arabian horse.

I would hate school again, flunk every possible subject, be betrayed by my best friend, be grossed out by my first kiss, dream of having long hair, organize my books on the shelves in my room in a certain order that is really a code.

A dog would again walk into my life and I would call her Joy and I would never love another dog that way until, thanks to time travel, some time in the past it's her again and me again.

Yes. I would again walk up to him and tell him that I like his tie and be perplexed that he does not reply, even after everything that happened after.

I would buy a small blue table to write on, do all the things I swore I'd never do and leave everything for love.

I would find my way to California and decide painfully, inexorably, that it is home, and stay, just like I did the first time around.

I'd date and walk into the hotel bar to find him sitting there waiting for me. He'd take me out to the desert to see monumental art illuminated by lightning and it would take days to get the dust out of our hair.

I'd jump at the chance to relive everything just how it happened.

I would not change a thing.

Proud Of Me

When I was about 16 I was a terrible student. I flunked almost every subject and managed to make it through the school year thanks to cramming through make up exams.

My parents were very angry at me.

During this time my relationship with them was strained. I slinked around and spent a lot of time in my room.

One evening my Dad knocked on my door and asked what I was listening to. We had a brief, inane conversation about music; the same one that has separated generations decade after decade.

My Dad stood there looking at me across this double chasm and that's when I knew.

No matter what I did or how badly I messed everything up, my parents would always be proud of me.

Hello, Chemistry

I was married for 15 years to a man I loved very much. After my divorce I felt I was pretty much done with things like "chemistry". Divorce made me feel half dead.

About a year later I was sitting at a bar with a guy I had just met. It was our first date, and it was going great. It was easy: easy flirting, easy conversation, easy laughter.

I had sent him a message after reading what I thought was a really funny online profile. At the very end he said *"reach out if you think you can beat me at arm wrestling."*

So there we were, ready to arm wrestle.

"I'm ready to arm wrestle" I said. I take my bets seriously.

"Are you sure you really want to do that?" he said.

"I am positive."

I set my elbow down on the table and stretched out my hand for him to take it.

He did.

I felt his strong, warm fingers circle mine and my memory of why chemistry is so important to people came back in less than an instant.

"YES. Hello, chemistry.

Hellooooo, chemistry.

Welcome back, you sexy thing."

Chemistry is ineffable. You can feel it when you like someone. You can feel it when you don't like the person very much at all. You can love someone very much and feel none.

You can feel the darn thing when you are absolutely not supposed to. (Which doesn't imply you have to act on it.)

Chemistry is unrelated to how much two people have in common.

Chemistry is a wonderful, free spirited beast and it comes and goes when it wants to.

You can't fabricate it. You can't summon it. You can't squelch it.

That's part of what makes it magic.

How I Know I Love Him

It's not that I would follow him anywhere or that he is what I measure truth against.

Not that I can see what's in his heart or that I blindly believe in him.

It's that every time I am presented with something good to eat I know I will give him the best bite.

Not Us

Not us
we are not like them
I told you so
this was your fault
your idea
you forgot again
were careless again
you never listen to me
you don't care anymore
how could you
we don't do this
not ever
I know only I can save you from me
only you can save me from you

Eternal

My father's house was concrete and thick slabs of polished hardwood.

For all its architectural grace, it was a fortress.

Many children grew within its walls; slept in its bedrooms, jumped from its bunk beds, played forbidden games of ball indoors and slid, often head first, down the wide white banister.

Any parent will tell you children can demolish any structure.

This one, massive, solid, remained unscathed and majestic through decades.

After we had all left and the house became too big for just one person my father sold a part of it — a smaller dwelling, equally immutable, that stood on other side of the garden. It had once been my bedroom and secret hideout.

The people who bought it claimed they would build their life within it and on my last trip to Mexico I looked out the window to find it had been razed.

I stood there so shocked I couldn't catch my breath.

How foolish of me to have conceived of concrete as permanent; to regard a building as a landmark.

We are conditioned to believe we leave something behind but

the concept of legacy is a fabrication.

I stood there stunned behind the curtain, considering.

If it's fallacious to think we leave something behind, then our birth is also an illusion.

We are all eternal.

Intelligent For What?

One day — I must have been around ten years old — a man asked my Dad if he was intelligent. (I have no idea why this even came about.)

To which my Dad replied *"Intelligent for what?"*

My Dad explained that he believed there where many different types of intelligence. That he was intelligent for some things, but not for others.

If someone asked me today if I was intelligent, my answer would be *"intelligent for what?"*

I honestly cannot say for sure if that's a good answer or not. But it would make my Dad grin (wherever he is) and that's enough for me.

Weird

Before I met my boyfriend, my fridge was impeccable.

My diet is almost vegetarian.

For the most part, I have an aversion to non vegetarian items.

I think quinoa is an excellent source of protein. I believe in the power of green juice. I have given up dairy — I put almond milk in my coffee and coconut milk in oatmeal.

After moving in Boyfriend, I came home one evening and opened the fridge. My jaw dropped when I saw a huge piece of steak on a plate.

It was adorned with a loving, gentle sprinkle of salt and black pepper.

What's weird about this incident is not that there was a BIG SLAB OF GLISTENING, RAW MEAT MARBLED WITH FAT in my refrigerator.

What's weird is that I found it adorable.

Saint

My Dad and I were in New York and had been walking for some time.

We hail a cab on Park Avenue and jump inside.

My Dad sees, on the floor of the back seat, a beautiful purse.

We look at each other.

My Dad grabs the purse and gingerly opens it (looking for ID.)

It was full of cash.

My Dad leans forward towards the driver.

Dad: *"Excuse me, where did you drop off the last person that was in this cab?"*

Driver: *"A couple of blocks from where I picked you up, Sir."*

Dad: *"We need to do a detour. Can you take us there?"*

Driver: *"Yes Sir."*

We drive for a couple of minutes and see a beautifully dressed woman, maybe in her 60s, agitatedly talking to her doorman.

Our cab, recognizing her, pulls over right next to them.

My Dad hops out of the car, strides over to the woman and

wordlessly hands her the purse.

The woman looks at the purse and looks at my Dad, speechless. My Dad hops back into the cab.

Dad: *"OK. Let's go."*

Driver: *"You, sir, are a saint."*

Moderately Grateful

My view of the world is black and white.

Conversations with Boyfriend go like this:

Me: *"I'm giving up coffee. I'll drink tea instead."*

Boyfriend: *"Why don't you just drink coffee sometimes?"*

Me: *"I'm sick of my hair. I'm going to cut it like Annie Lennox."*

Boyfriend: *"Why don't you get a trim and see how you feel?"*

Every time he gives me an un-extreme option it blows my mind that it's even available to me. It's just not how I think.

I'd declare this perspective fills me with such gratitude my heart could burst; but he'd feel more comfortable if I instead stated I'm moderately grateful for his perspective.

Our Own Higgs Boson

As a lover of structure I wish I could pinpoint the second it all began.

Perhaps it was when I first came across your photographs and captions. Their selection betrayed an urgency I was convinced was visible only to me.

Or maybe it was before we met. You were tugging on me years ago, back when I first realized it was time to leave him and start over.

Maybe it was reading the list of things you couldn't live without and knowing I could easily ensure your survival by providing an endless array of good Japanese knives and a life replete with serendipity.

It could have been later too. After I told you on the sidewalk that I would never get on a motorcycle with a stranger. After the homeless man in the gas station assured me that you were a keeper. Or later, after you grimaced the first time I called you my boyfriend.

Or yesterday, when I realized I both need space and need you.

It's possible too that the answer doesn't exist. That there's a missing piece out there with the potential to elucidate not only how and when our universe began but how it works and how our most elemental pieces fit together.

It would interpret why the currently abstract matter that constitutes our relationship has mass. And how, combined with gravity, it lends weight to what we are building.

Maybe some day we will find it, and it will explain everything.

Overprotective

My dad is on his death bed, eyes closed, liver distended. I'm lying next to him, his hand in mine, and I'm not even sure if he can hear me.

"Will you take care of me from wherever you go?" I ask.

His eyes remain closed but he smirks.

"I will take care of you and intervene even when you wouldn't want me to."

He was always overprotective. How silly of me to assume death would change that.

I'm Being Erased

I don't sleep well here but when I do I dream the thick black outlines of me are being erased. This is a messy undertaking. It leaves eraser residue all over the page. Soon, very soon, I will become invisible.

I only wear gray threadbare sweatpants and write long winded stories on the shower door with a felt tip pen. Then, I stand back and watch the jet of hot water make the ink run until not a single word is legible.

I wake up at dawn without ever setting an alarm clock. Alarmless is what I have become. Mornings hurt, like a dry thud or a weight, despite the clear, white light that streams in through the skylight I have stared up at since I was a child.

I lie there, and know that the routine that engulfs me is a safe haven, necessary. But it's rubbing me out. The only thing that makes you feel alive is what is destined to kill you; and yet what is safe obliterates you. Poison and antidote, indiscernible.

Before swinging my legs out of bed I wonder if I should examine myself, like one would immediately after a car accident. I assume I'd want to check my most fragile places first, so I ask an expert in crashes if this is what one does. His sensible advice is to start where the pain is. Except, I don't know where the pain is. It's a thread, and it's sticky and thick and black and it runs through everything, and it's making a mess, just like erasing my outline would, leaving residue all over the page.

Another Me

There are 40 billion planets like Earth out there, and those are only the ones we know about in a universe that is infinite.

With those odds, I guess it's possible there is another me out there, drinking coffee her boyfriend brewed, writing and wondering if I exist.

Tip Extravagantly

Two men are sitting across from me on the bus. They are speaking Spanish.

First man: *"If I tell you what happened yesterday, you won't believe me."*

Second man: *"What?"*

First man: *"We were at the site. At noon the boss said it was lunch time. We sat down to a huge plate of hot food and that red wine that they serve in glasses."*

Second man stares.

First man: *"When we were done we all got another plate. I'm still full."*

Second man stares.

First man: *"Then, he gave us each an envelope and said "this is so you can go get coffee, on such a cold day". In it was $50."*

Second man's jaw drops.

First man: *"$50. For coffee."*

They look at each other, then burst out laughing.

Tip generously.

Misfortune

I was having dinner alone in a restaurant in San Francisco. The tables were close together.

There was a couple right next to me, and she asked him to talk dirty to her in a language she liked the sound of but didn't understand.

Unfortunately, I did.

The Lies We Tell

I will always take care of you
I will never
this is forever
this is constant
under control
I am alone
nobody would understand
this is unequivocal
absolute
unsolvable
unforgivable
that is impossible
this is a principle
a cornerstone
The Truth
my Truth
there are two sides to every story

(two sides couldn't quite cover any story)

Built For Hardship

I am from Mexico. My boyfriend is from Montreal.

The last time we visited Montreal I opened the curtains to look at the sky and the window was lined with icicles.

Icicles.

We stepped outside and just as I was thinking *"I am going to die"* Boyfriend said *"Oh, wow! It's not so bad!"*

After a few days in his beautiful city I confessed I might not survive the harsh, inhuman winter conditions. He reminded me it was mid-April.

The secret to making it through winter is wearing the right clothes, and learning how to layer them.

For people used to seasons this is second nature. Not for me.

I explain to Boyfriend that I was built for hardship. Whenever we go to his stunningly beautiful country I can be found cowering in a corner somewhere, reluctant to wander outside.

That's when I point out I was built for hardship, but not the weather kind. Other hardship. Not winter. Not even spring.

Sour

A woman gets on the bus and sits next to me.

Her curly hair comes down to her waist.

She has purple fingernails and big rings.

I compliment her on her vintage coat and she gives me this look: bewildered, then sour.

She turns away and opens her book. *"How to Win Friends and Influence People."*

But First, Acceptance

Finding happiness is a journey.

A good way to start on this complex, wonderful process is to take a good look at what you are and *accept* it. From this place of loving acceptance you can find people like you who define happiness in the same way.

You stop asking questions like: *"Am I normal? Is there something wrong with me? Should I try to be something other than what I am?"* (The answers are: yes, no and please no.)

The worst way to start on this complex, wonderful process is to force yourself to be something you are not. You will be met with the strongest, most primal, most desperate internal resistance. You will end up surrounded by the wrong people (for you). You will (read this and remember it always) condemn yourself to perpetual inadequacy. You will wake up one morning wondering how on Earth you ended up in the wrong life.

Improving yourself — striving to be a better person — is essential to happiness.

Changing yourself — trying to be something you aren't, will make you angry, bitter, resentful, hopeless, lonely.

Believe me when I tell you who you already are is perfect. Go find that. Accept that. Love that. Amplify it. Be proud of it. Hold it up so others like you can find you.

Secret

I keep a secret from you
Unwillingly
It's not elaborate or curious
It's not intentional
It's not associated to betrayal or deceit

It involves growing old
My veins showing blue through my skin

It's about how I know I need to take responsibility

How I suspect that in the end
I will have to do this on my own

Ant Sized

When I'm all tangled up in a common, daily struggle, I go somewhere with a view.

Yesterday, while waiting for the elevator, I looked out the window down onto the street below. I was up so high that people looked small, like toys, with their briefcases and sneakers and coats flapping in the autumn wind.

I wonder, how many times does someone see me from a distance?

I don't really mean watching me as an individual, as someone that has been attached to a specific identity. I don't mean attraction or curiosity or being noticed, but rather the opposite of relevance.

How many times am I, say, on a ferry on the San Francisco Bay while someone is looking at the boat from a car driving across the Golden Gate Bridge?

How many times does someone lying on the beach see the plane I'm in slowly move across the arch of blue sky in his span of vision?

How many times has someone taken a photograph and caught a fragment of me as I move across the frame? How many albums do I live in as even less than a stranger, the tip of my shoe intruding on a picture, a brown blur caused by a curly strand of my hair ruining an otherwise perfect family shot?

How many times does someone look down and notice people look like toys, with their briefcases and sneakers and coats flapping in the autumn wind; and realize they not only seem small, but trivial, deceived in their sweet sense of self importance, foolish, really, to be hurrying along as if their efforts really amounted to anything?

What I mean is, how many times is one of those minuscule, ant sized people way down below me?

The Light In His Eyes

One of the best things my Dad did for me growing up — which partially shaped my regard for myself — was the way he lit up when I walked into the room.

Before dying he was very, very sick, with colon cancer and a type of dementia that greatly affected his short term memory.

From one moment to the next he did not remember I was there.

So he gave me that same look of absolute delight pretty much every time he closed his eyes and opened them again.

Ferocious Love

My Dad always loved telling me how he met my mom.

As he began showing signs of dementia this was one of the stories he would insist on repeating.

At every telling it would include more and more details about their sex life.

"Dad!" I would say *"Please stop! Ugh! Parents never have sex!"*
He found this hilarious. *"How do you think you were made?"*

A few weeks before his death he insisted on putting me through a conversation about how amazing sex had been with my mother.

Ack.

I asked him to stop. *"Please."* I covered my ears. I sang. *"LALALALALALA."* I shook my head.

Nothing deterred him.

I think that the point he wanted to get across was that I was conceived with unimaginable passion and ferocious love.

While now that he's gone I hold this in my heart, there are parts of the story I wish I could un-hear.

As Long As You Are Here

As long as you are here
there will never be a drought
no shortage of things to write about
my new lip gloss
the smell of taxis in Canada
the shape of the pasta we tried in the restaurant near our place
That dish you made for us the first time you cooked in our
kitchen
back pain and how it's changed
the light in the photograph of all of us around the dinner table
that looks like a Rembrandt
the metal spirals of barbed wire lined with razors
installed on top of fences in countries everywhere
the virtues and pitfalls of orange paint and expensive furniture
wanting new things
parts of me that still surprise me
all the things I miss
do we ever really get to know ourselves

Big Garbage Bag

Boyfriend and I hung out with a six year old friend a few weekends ago.

We developed a complex, carefully orchestrated plan involving hunting and gathering ingredients, mixing and baking and finally, triumphantly assembling and eating 3D cookie dinosaurs, but that was not the highlight.

The most shrieks of joy resulted from the two of them dashing downstairs to the garbage room and hollering at me on the third floor so I would, on command, release the trash bag down the chute.

Happiness lurks everywhere. Even in garbage bags.

The Advice I'd Give Me

My father was a strong, authoritative, dictatorial, loving character with a big, complicated family.

Towards the end of his life he suffered from dementia.

It was about five years ago that the symptoms he was presenting could no longer be explained away as idiosyncrasies.

Witnessing his fear and inability to make decisions was indescribably terrifying.

He died a year ago today.

Losing a parent changes you forever. Losing him slowly, watching him become a shell of himself, created so much anxiety within me that it was like experiencing my worst nightmare on constant replay.

If I had the chance I would tell myself to discard worry and anxiety. It accomplishes nothing.

Most of the things I feared would happen did not.

For all the awful things that did, I was better equipped to deal with them than I thought I was.

My father raised us well.

"Don't suffer more than you have to, Dushka. You are stronger than you think. It's impossible to see how now, but everything will work out. You just wait and see."

238

The Bottom Of The Box

Ever since the first time I heard this story I was told hope was at the bottom of Pandora's box.

I now think something got lost in translation.

Hope implies the expectation that things will turn out a desired way.

I believe that what we find is instead a mix of trust + faith + surrender. A blind sense that it will all work out even if we don't yet know exactly how.

The gift at the bottom of her box is faith.

I'll Run Into You

Behind me on the bus:

Her: *"I'd love to see you more often!"*

Him: *"Yeah."*

Her: *"Cool! When?"*

Him: *"I'll text you."*

Her: *"Do you have my number?"*

Him: *"Don't need it. I'll run into you."*

Her: *"Oh, wow! That sounds perfect!"*

He flips his hair back, gets up, exits bus.

She sighs.

I would have given her sound advice.

But she wouldn't have listened.

Better Than Happiness

Yellow makes me happy. And chocolate. And very soft clothes. A sunny afternoon and the luxury of extra time. Saturday morning. Coffee. A beautiful view.

Seeing my Dad deathly sick did not make me happy. It was, in fact, torture. I wanted very much to run in the other direction. A person I loved was suffering and in pain, but also had dementia, which came with aggression, paranoia and nightmarish hallucinations.

But here is the thing: sitting next to my Dad when he died, holding his hand, is one of the best things I've ever done. In exchange for that, I'd turn Saturdays into Mondays. I would never again drink coffee. I'd book my calendar solid and wear scratchy sweaters. I would give up yellow.

Longing

For the feeling after yoga to last all day
Grounded and peaceful
for one night of deep uninterrupted sleep
for a dark corner in a hotel bar (or any sacred place) where your
hand might touch my arm again
for a pause button (I could have said rewind)
a stop button
for the way things used to be
back when my parents had superpowers
framed my paintings
tucked me in tight
for how fresh everything looks
for travel
for music
my headphones
for a place to hide
or not need to
for good food
we never shared
but most of all
for Sundays with you

Living Alone

I love living alone.

I love the silence, beauty and symmetry of my house.

I love sleeping in the middle of the bed, sometimes diagonally.

I love setting up my own rhythm, reading far into the night, writing early in the morning, opening the fridge and calling an apple with peanut butter "dinner".

I love getting a bowl of fruit and flowers for the dining room table.

When I wake up on Sunday mornings I lie there still and feel the cadence of my own heartbeats and know I have a beautiful day stretched out before me, with a sky that is blue and crisp and anything but empty.

I think everyone should live alone at least once in their life.

If He Was Here

My Dad died about a year ago.

I lost him gradually. He had very slow progressing dementia for years; then died exactly two years to the day of a colon cancer diagnosis.

My point is that I had time, and that I told him everything. I told him he was the best father in the world, and that I loved him. I repeated this every time we spoke and I said it again the day I watched him die.

If he appeared before me today I would tell him what I know he would immediately want to be filled in on: I would tell him about each one of my siblings.

My oldest brother has turned out to be such a good father, of the two most adorable kids. My sister is the bravest person I know, intelligent and strong. And my youngest brother is one of my favorite people on Earth. I would talk a lot about him. (Yes Dad. He is engaged, just like you predicted.)

There are days when I yearn so badly to fill my father in on all the shenanigans my siblings get into that it actually hurts. He would be so delighted. He would be so proud.

I would also tell him how my mom is doing. They got a divorce when I was three, and for the past 43 years the first thing he always did — even as the dementia worsened — was ask me about her. Even though they visited each other several times a week.

Everyone misses you Dad. And you made amazing human beings. Thank you for my family. Thank you for my siblings.

My Mother's Lies

Whenever my brother and I fought, which was pretty much all the time, my mother would scream

"CHILDREN STOP IT RIGHT NOW UNLESS YOU WANT ME TO SLAM YOUR HEADS TOGETHER UNTIL YOUR TEETH COME OUT ON THE OTHER SIDE OF YOUR HEAD!"

This terrified us for years.

When we turned around 8 (him) and 11 (me) we decided it would in fact be incredibly cool to have teeth in the back of our heads.

Naturally, we put in considerable additional effort to fight extra rambunctiously.

My mother never actually slammed our heads together.

Terrible Liar

My father and I are walking around the garden.

He has dementia which manifests mostly in a sharp loss of short term memory.

Our conversations are mind-numbingly repetitive. I listen to the same things over and over and struggle to determine what is better: the truth, or kindness? Being blunt or trying to take the edge off how afraid we all are?

We have a history of telling each other everything so I agonize over this in every one of our conversations.

He asks a question related to his medical treatment and I provide an answer I consider both swift and smooth.

He gives me a sideways glance.

My Dad — who is in such an advanced stage of dementia that I fear for the moment he will turn around and not know who I am — says *"Oh, Dushka. For a person with such startling clarity of thought, you have always been a terrible liar."*

Despite repeated attempts, I never knew how to deceive my parents.

Hiding Places

I have no curtains so it can't hide behind them

doesn't like my car
loves airplanes
not public places

is never idle on the sofa
or twisted between my sheets

it does like it under the bed
outside
loves the beach
but not on a sunny day

it sometimes sneaks into my purse

I often find some in the watering can
the bottom drawer of the refrigerator
near where I hang my bathing suit to dry
under the kitchen counter
the backyard
inside my boots
in the pockets of my jeans
tangled in the laces of my hiking shoes

these are the places where I find
what to write about

Confidence

Boyfriend and I met online so naturally we both had profiles up on the dating site.

After a few dates, the following conversation took place:

Boyfriend: *"I just want you to know I am no longer going to be dating other people. I only want to date you."*

Me: *"But, but, but it's so fast! I don't know if I'm ready! I already have other dates set up!"*

Boyfriend: *"Dushka. I never asked you to stop seeing other people. I just said I wasn't going to see other people. You can do anything you want."*

A couple of days later I went on a coffee date with someone else and right away thought *"But, he's not Boyfriend."*

This is how Boyfriend ruined dating for me.

Instead Of One

It's time to go.

My sister-in-law calls the kids over.

"Guys! Auntie Dushka is leaving! Come say goodbye!"

My nephew, possibly the cutest kid on this planet and all neighboring planets, turns to look at me, forlorn.

He shuffles over, head hanging.

"Auntie Dushka."

"Yes, sweetheart?"

"When you come next time, can you please bring me two gifts instead of one?"

Defying Stephen King

I walked into class on my first day of college feeling edgy and disoriented to find Carla sitting on the other side of the room, under the window. She looked right at me and flashed me a smile. More than feeling like she was greeting a stranger I felt like she was recognizing someone she had always known and was happy to see. I walked over and sat next to her.

Her company was easy; she laughed often and loudly. We defined loyalty similarly, and agreed on what we felt was most important, even as that evolved. From that day, she set up permanent residence in my heart and now, 25 years later, still firmly holds the title of Best Friend.

"I never had any friends later on like the ones I had when I was 12," wrote Stephen King in Stand by Me. I asked my Dad if this could possibly be true. He nodded. *"Life gets in the way"* he said. *"You have less time and other priorities."*

I won't be that kind of adult, I vowed. I don't want to ever become a person who feels she doesn't have time for friends.

And then I got busy.

I got picky too. Arriving at a restaurant on time or an ability to make and stick to agreed upon commitments became a critical requirement. If I didn't have time, I definitely did not have time for flaky.

In my late twenties and thirties my life revolved around moving to a new country, working in a demanding, full time job that involved building teams, and being a good wife. I didn't have time for much else.

And then I got a divorce.

I told my friend Amit that the hardest thing as a single woman in her 40s was opening my eyes after the alarm went off and determining in those first seconds how I was going to get through the day. He proceeded to call me every morning at 6:45.

I was vexed to realize that I had somehow bought into the notion that I didn't have time, that I had more important things to do, that friends were not a priority. If you tell yourself "it's too hard", that becomes reality. In other words, I voluntarily closed myself off to one of the most enriching, heart-filling, affirming parts of life.

My friend Andrea said it best: *"Friends, like sleep, are an essential yet undervalued aspect of our existence."*

And then my Dad got sick — fatally sick — and he didn't have many friends come by to see him. The end of his life forced me to more carefully evaluate what I was doing with mine.

I think every day about defying Stephen King. I try to be open to the delicate serendipity of making new friends. I remind myself to embrace people for exactly who they are and watch with wonder how they show up their way, not mine.

I also go out of my way to spend time with all the friends I made back when it felt like love, back when I saw my best friend Carla's big eyes in the light of that window. Back when the two of us spent whole afternoons hanging out on the couch laughing without it ever occurring to either of us it would one day be necessary to make more elaborate plans.

Spatial Impediment

It's not just that I have no sense of direction. It's that I never know where I am.

If I have an important meeting to go to I can easily prepare the content. It's getting there that causes me the most stress.

If a navigation system or map advises me to *"head East"* I stand on the sidewalk in utter paralysis.

If we are at the MET and my friend says *"I will meet you at the store"* I have to use my phone to get there or I will get turned around.

My friends and loved ones are amused by my faulty spatial impairment. I consider it one of my greatest handicaps.

I wish I had a sense of direction.

Crushingly Romantic

Boyfriend is cooking. I'm walking around the kitchen.

"Life is so impossible to predict" I say, *"with its twists and turns and surprises. What do you think are the chances that we will actually grow old together?"*

"Dushka" Boyfriend says, *"we're already old."*

Destiny

Ah, destiny. What a terrible, beautiful, dangerous word.

It implies that your life is already written, the course of events predetermined.

The concept is tempting if I consider its promise: that it could be possible for my purpose and I to somehow spot each other across a noisy, crowded room and fall irrevocably into each other's arms.

Or, the implication that I could meet a man at bar late one Tuesday evening and know that he was "destined" to be in my life forever.

I don't believe in destiny. I instead believe in my own power.

I define destiny as the path I carve for myself with the decisions that I make (and a few other spicy, delicious ingredients.)

My favorite definition of "destiny" was written by Ambrose Bierce.

"Destiny: A tyrant's authority for crime and a fool's excuse for failure."

The Right Decision

It's easy to assume that the right decisions will lead to the desired outcome.

The flaw in this thinking is that the desired outcome depends on many, many different variables (many of which you might not know about) beyond your decision making.

Therefore, it's possible to make all the right decisions and arrive at an outcome other than what was desired.

The way to know you've made the right decisions, to me, is what you're left with over time: peace of mind, a healthy relationship with those you love, being happy with who you are are all examples of the mark of a series of good decisions.

You know you've made a bad decision or a series of bad decisions when you don't like where your life is at and you wish you could start over.

(Bonus tip: you can always start over.)

So Much To Learn

A young guy and an old man are sitting beside me on the bus, speaking Spanish.

"To be healthy" the old man says *"your cells have to reproduce."* He continues. *"Cells are about 4.5 centimeters, at least the long ones, and look like veins. For them to reproduce you have to have sex. This is why old ladies get sick and die. They're no longer interested in sex so their cells can't reproduce."*

The young guy is impassive.

"Life's nice" adds the old man. *"But there's so much to learn to understand how to live it."*

Be Careful

I try to stop.

I don't want to say it, but I can't help myself.

I tell my brother *"be careful, be careful"* and he looks so exasperated — *"Do you think I want to get hurt? That if you say nothing I won't be?"*

"I love you," I blurt. What it really means is I love you.

And now I've made him even more uncomfortable.

Neither of us know what to do with me.

Books or eBooks?

I am a book lover, and my ex-husband gave me the first Kindle ever to exist for my birthday some years ago.

I was skeptical at first. Reluctant. (OK — I looked at him perplexed and asked *"Why did you buy me this? How could you do this to me?"*)

Since that brief, myopic moment, I've discovered Kindle is not a gadget for gadget lovers — it's a gadget for book lovers. It's sleek and light, yet unassuming. The screen is sharp, high-resolution electronic paper (so, technically, not a screen but a surface.)

It's very easy to use. You don't need cables or a computer. There is no need to do any syncing.

If you're reading a book and come across a word you don't know the meaning of, you can look it up. This has prompted me to look up words even when I do know what they mean, because it's so quick and easy I can satisfy my curiosity about, say, their etymology.

My favorite part: If I'm holding my Kindle and you recommend a good book, I can find it, download it and start reading it in less than a minute.

Although it claims to use cell phone technology I think it's a combination of pixie dust and telepathy. It's not that I don't understand how it works. It's that it feels like nothing less than magic to see the book you want in your possession in less time than it would take you to find your car keys.

I can receive the New York Times (or any major international newspaper, magazine or blog) every morning before it even is available in print.

Kindle saves paper (there is nothing to print), and if yours breaks and you send it back to them they recycle it. It isn't cheap, but hard cover books cost around $25, and the same book in the kindle version is $9.99.

Books that aren't the latest bestsellers can be yours (in under a minute) for less than that. For example, after running into a great quote (*"it's a poor sort of memory that only works backward"*), I decided I needed to re-read Alice in Wonderland and paid $2 for it.

President Obama's inaugural address is mine to read whenever I want, I don't have to carry the newspaper clipping with me, and it was less than half a dollar.

On Kindle, you can not only read, you can download free samples (roughly the first chapter) of almost every book you'd like to check out, acquire books at the speed of light and carry 200 books in a device that's less than half the size of a small laptop; you can also take notes, "clip" pages and archive them (in order), and listen to music. You can also use the "search" feature to find anything online. (What are the Seven Wonders of the Modern World? Give me a minute!)

To all you naysayers who insist you must hold a book, turn its smooth pages and smell that clean, new paper smell, I say to you: I understand with all my heart.

But, why would such a convenient device and a book be mutually exclusive? Use Kindle for travel, and read books at home.

Guy Talk

Boyfriend went out to drinks with a guy friend. We have been wondering about him: his job is frustrating him, his relationship is rocky.

Boyfriend comes home three hours later, holding his motorcycle helmet. He smells of Scotch and gasoline.

"How did it go?" I ask. *"Is he OK? Does he have interviews lined up? Is he moving out? Update me!"*

"I don't know" he replies. *"We sat at the bar and grunted."*

Life Lesson

My brother and I are yelling at each other over something. Anything. Everything. I think this time it was that we both wanted to sit next to my mom.

She turns around and glares at me.

"Dushka" she says over the shrill screams. *"Just do me a favor and let your brother sit here."*

"But mom!" I say, summoning the brand of indignance only available to a seven old *"it's not fair!"*

"The world isn't fair kid" she replies. *"Deal with it."*

A Force For Good

If you want to take over the world, marshal all your intelligence, your force, your grit, your master planning, your plotting, conniving, manipulating, colluding and conspiring and resolve once and for all to use all your powers for good.

The instant the bad guys in James Bond films go wrong is when they decide to be a force for evil.

Despite the suspense, excitement and temporary, fleeting triumph, in the end good will always win.

Antidotes To A Bad Day

A yoga class. Breathing and moving through the poses. *Ahhhhhhh.*

Calling someone I love. Not to talk about whatever is going badly with my day but about what's new with them. It changes the grouchy movie playing inside my head.

And the mega antidote that decimates any residue of ick: heading out somewhere with a sweeping view. Looking at things from above never fails to put everything in perspective.

How To Be Remembered

I think about this a lot, mostly because my dad died and he was wonderful and I so very much want him to be remembered.

The most common options:

A tree, a book, a child.

Other possibilities:

A forest. (He deserves a forest.)

Donating all your books to an underprivileged public library (we donated all of his.) Money to pay for someone's education.

Love: the love you give remains forever in the heart of others. (I carry him with me always.)

Help pulling someone up in any way available to you (for example, be a mentor to someone; or give people tips that would have helped you.)

Do many, many good deeds and request that they all be paid forward.

I should warn you, though, that all this postpones the inevitable, which is that eventually none of this will matter and we will all be forgotten.

But I think it's fun to try.

Talk Dirty To Me

Boyfriend: *"Hi."*

Me: *"Hi!"*

Boyfriend: *"Good morning."*

Me: *"Good morning."*

Boyfriend: *"Are you ready for coffee?"*

Me: *"YES"*

Boyfriend: *"With almond milk?"*

Me: *"YES FROTHY"*

Boyfriend: *"How about breakfast?"*

Me: *"YES breakfast!"*

Boyfriend: *"Oatmeal? Eggs?"*

Me: *"Ooooh! Eggs! Eggs!"*

Boyfriend: *"How about fried eggs on a vegetable hash? I can chop some onions, celery, carrots, jalapeño peppers -"*

Me: *"YES JALAPEÑOS YEAH"*

Boyfriend: *"I can add some sweet potatoes"*

Me: *"OOOOH SWEEET POTATO YUM"*

Boyfriend: *"I'll make the yolk oozy —"*

Me: *swoon*

Space

I need space
Not a room or a house
But a swath of the milky way
Not a backyard a national park
Not elbow room dream room
Not a puddle an ocean
Not a line in the sand the split of land from sky
I need my eyes to see as far as they can
I don't know how someone so small can need something so big

But I do

My Very Own Word

Walking around San Francisco I saw a woman sitting at a desk in front of an old typewriter.

A sign next to her on the sidewalk read *"A word = two dollars."*

I sat down.

She looked at me.

Her: *"How can I help you?"*

Me: *"I'd like a word."*

Her: *"OK. Tell me about yourself."*

Me: "*Everything is changing nothing is in its place I know what's right but I'm scared sometimes I want a word to remind me of that place that's mine where I belong where I will always be safe I love words I can carry it with me I don't know what else to say.*"

She takes a piece of paper, inserts it into the typewriter, types something, pulls it out and hands it to me. I pay her and leave.

A few blocks away I open it.

"Precipice".

Why Love Exists

Boyfriend wakes up in the morning looking like a disheveled bear that has been hibernating.

His T-shirt is wrinkled, his hair is sticking out in every possible direction, his eyes are groggy and he grunts and growls all the way to the coffee maker.

I can't tell you how absolutely gorgeous he looks.

Perfection is not within the realm of possibility for humans — not in the people that we love, not in the relationships we build, not in the things that we do — and that's why love exists.

About the Author

After more than 20 years in the communications industry I noticed a theme.

It is very difficult to articulate who you are and what you do.

This holds true for both companies and for individuals.

For companies, this is an impediment to the development of an identity, a reputation, a brand.

It makes it hard for your customers to see how you are different from your competitors.

For individuals, in a new world order of personal brands, it makes it hard to develop one that feels real.

This is what I do. I help companies and people put into simple terms who they are, what they do, and where to go next.

My work comes to life through message development, presentation training, media training and personal brand development.

It comes to life through executive coaching, workshops and public speaking.

It comes to life through what I write.

My first book is called "How to be Ferociously Happy". This is my second book.

I live in San Francisco with Boyfriend, who after five years still makes me coffee every morning.

Made in the USA
San Bernardino, CA
07 November 2016